Your Perfect Swing

Jim Suttie

Human Kinetics

Library of Congress Cataloging-in-Publication Data

Suttie, James K., 1946-
  Your perfect swing / Jim Suttie.
      p. cm.
  Includes index.
  ISBN 0-7360-3423-4 (soft cover)
  1. Swing (Golf) I. Title.
  GV979.S9S85 2005
  796.352'3--dc22

                                            2004030640

ISBN-10: 0-7360-3423-4
ISBN-13: 978-0-7360-3423-4

Copyright © 2006 by James K. Suttie

Acquisitions Editor: Martin Barnard; **Developmental Editor:** Jennifer L. Walker; **Assistant Editors:** Mandy Maiden and Kim Thoren; **Copyeditor:** John Wentworth; **Proofreader:** Ann M. Augspurger; **Indexer:** Bobbi Swanson; **Permission Manager:** Toni Harte; **Graphic Designer:** Nancy Rasmus; **Graphic Artist:** Tara Welsch; **Photo Manager:** Dan Wendt; **Cover Designer:** Keith Blomberg; **Photographer (cover):** Chuck Cherney; **Photographer (interior):** photos on pages 37 (figure 3.2a), 38 (figure 3.5), 39–40, 41 (figures 3.9 and 3.10), 42 (figure 3.11), 46, 51–52, 53 (figure 3.30), 56–58, 61, 66, 69 (figure 3.52, a and b), 76, 82–85, 87, 88 (figure 4.8), 90–91, 95–97, 104 (figure 4.25, a and b), 106–107, 113, 116–117, 120, 123, 171, and 188–189 © Bob Klein; photos on pages 36, 37 (figures 3.2b and 3.3), 38 (figure 3.4), 41 (figure 3.8), 42 (figure 3.12), 43, 45, 47–49, 53 (figure 3.29), 54, 59, 62 (figure 3.40), 63–64, 69 (figures 3.53 and 3.54), 70–71, 74, 80, 86, 88 (figure 4.9), 92, 98, 100–103, 104 (figure 4.24, a–c), 105, 108, 114, 130, 132–133, 135, 141, 143, 145 (figure 6.17), 151, 153, 157 (figure 6.26), 158 (figure 6.31), 162–163 (figure 6.35), 165–167, 168 (figure 6.45), 169, 172, 178 (figure 7.5), 184, 185 (figure 7.12), 186, 187 (figure 7.15), 190–191, 195, and 196 © Chuck Cherney; and photos on pages 4–5, 62 (figures 3.41–3.43), 118–119, 127, 128–129, 137–138, 140, 142, 144, 145 (figure 6.18), 146–148, 152, 154, 157 (figures 6.27 and 6.28), 158 (figures 6.29 and 6.30), 160–161, 162–163 (figure 6.34), 164, 168 (figure 6.44), 175–177, 178 (figure 7.4), 180–181, 183, 185 (figure 7.13), 187 (figure 7.16), and 189 (figure 7.18) © William Daniels; **Art Manager and Illustrator:** Kareema McLendon-Foster; **Printer:** United Graphics

Human Kinetics books are available at special discounts for bulk purchase. Special editions or book excerpts can also be created to specification. For details, contact the Special Sales Manager at Human Kinetics.

Printed in the United States of America   10 9 8 7 6 5 4 3 2

Human Kinetics
Web site: www.HumanKinetics.com

United States: Human Kinetics
P.O. Box 5076
Champaign, IL 61825-5076
800-747-4457
e-mail: humank@hkusa.com

Canada: Human Kinetics
475 Devonshire Road Unit 100
Windsor, ON N8Y 2L5
800-465-7301 (in Canada only)
e-mail: orders@hkcanada.com

Europe: Human Kinetics
107 Bradford Road
Stanningley
Leeds LS28 6AT, United Kingdom
+44 (0) 113 255 5665
e-mail: hk@hkeurope.com

Australia: Human Kinetics
57A Price Avenue
Lower Mitcham, South Australia 5062
08 8277 1555
e-mail: liaw@hkaustralia.com

New Zealand: Human Kinetics
Division of Sports Distributors NZ Ltd.
P.O. Box 300 226 Albany
North Shore City
Auckland
0064 9 448 1207
e-mail: info@humankinetics.co.nz

I dedicate this book to my wife, Sandra. If she didn't continue to encourage me, this manuscript would not be printed. I owe everything to her.

Contents

Acknowledgments

I would like to thank the following people who contributed to the completion of this book. First, my wife Sandra, who encouraged me to keep at it. Second, the photographers and friends who contributed to this book: Bill Daniels, Bob Klein, and Chuck Cherney. Third, Martin Barnard, Acquisitions Editor at Human Kinetics, for his patience. Thanks to James Robertson for helping with the rewrite of the text and to Dr. James Sudmier for his help reviewing the material. Thanks also to my friend Chip Beck who was instrumental in encouraging me and supporting me in writing this book. Finally, thanks to all my golf students who put up with my constant questions.

Introduction

I'm convinced that most golfers truly want to swing better. As golfers, we sit up and take notice of the well-oiled swing of Ernie Els, the explosive power of Tiger Woods, and the laser-like ball-striking accuracy of Annika Sorenstam. I've been teaching golf professionally for over 30 years and still get a thrill from watching the swings on the golf tours. If you're one of those players who wants to change your game, make improvements, and really dig in and do the work, we can work together through the lessons in this book to improve your game and keep on improving it for years to come.

A Unique Teaching Approach

First, you might be wondering, "How is this experience going to differ from the tips and quick-fix lessons I've had in the past, or from the other how-to golf books already out on the shelves?" Your lessons are going to be different because they are all about *you* and helping you customize and maintain your own golf swing. You won't simply be cast into the "one size fits all" golf swing method that predominates golf instruction and forces you to adapt to a single model and way of teaching.

Working with literally thousands of students over the years has taught me how to empower you as your own best coach. Learning to customize the golf swing, and becoming your own best golf coach, is working successfully for thousands of golfers around the world. The aspirations of players I work with range from wanting to win a club championship, breaking 100 consistently, or playing on one of the professional golf tours to reducing handicaps and simply getting more enjoyment out of the time on the golf course.

The Development of the Customized Approach

The dedicated golfer is the audience I had in mind when I sat down to write this book. I realized that although top pros such as Tiger and Annika seem to be getting better over time, the dedicated, novice player seems to be standing still, or moving backward. I've learned from studying the playing statistics and from the frustration voiced by so many golfers out there that most golfers are not improving. My teaching career has been devoted to the firm belief that it's possible for you to make dramatic improvements in relatively short order and increase your enjoyment of the game.

In fact, I've made it a lifelong career goal to learn as much as possible about all golf swings so that I could cure even your most subtle swing flaws. I even went to the extreme of completing a doctoral degree in biomechanics. My major motivation for going back to school was that I couldn't find a satisfactory biomechanical explanation for the golf swing that players could actually understand and use. Part of the problem is that golf is unique from throwing a baseball, shooting a basketball, shooting a hockey puck, kicking a soccer ball, or even tossing a football around in the back yard. A better model was needed to help adjust to the fact that golf is an underhanded game that must be played from the side of the ball. Stop and think about that uniqueness for just a second!

As a component of my work, I therefore set out to develop a biomechanical model that would help you understand a mechanically sound swing. I started my work in creating a model swing by filming the movements of the leading tour players. I filmed them in slow motion, digitized their swings, and used those digital images to create the swing of an "ideal" professional golfer. Once my mechanically sound model was generated and refined, I went about the business of teaching it to my students.

In the beginning of using this method, I had very good results—especially with beginners; however, over the years that followed I began noticing that this ideal professional swing model wasn't working for *everybody*. Many of my students found themselves falling into their same old unproductive habits after a few months away from my teaching. It was nearly impossible for many of my students to maintain the "on-plane" swing the way my model was directing them to. It took me a while to realize that my students' bodies, physical proportions, and equipment didn't match the characteristics of any ideal model I had developed—or ever could develop. I concluded that one of the game's historical teaching failures revolves around the fact that we were teaching the same swing to students with widely diverse body types and mental approaches to the game. Golfers come equipped with unique bodies, as well as individualized swing styles, thought processes, levels of flexibility, power sources, motivation, and a myriad of other influences that affect their swings and the way they play the game.

I realized I had the teaching formula backward. Rather than teaching a swing that used individual traits to a player's advantage, I'd been forcing all of the unique swing styles of my students into a rigid model. It was like trying to fit all golfers with the same size golf shoe. My teaching technique was suffering from some insurmountable disadvantages. What I figured out in the process from developing to implementing my strategy with real live students was that my computerized model had been, and remains today, an effective *starting and learning reference point* for helping players customize their swings, but not the be-all end-all answer for every golfer.

The Customized Method and the Key Swing Models

In order to "correct" and revamp my teaching strategy, I began by identifying several model swing systems. It's these swing systems you'll learn to identify and apply throughout your reading here. They are the mechanically sound swing model, the pro tour model, and the customized swing model.

We start in chapter 1 with the biomechanical swing model I developed through research and computer simulation. I refer to this as the *mechanically sound swing model*. This is the swing you'll learn to identify, work toward, and gauge your progress against over the course of your study. It's also the easiest swing for you to maintain once you've learned it because it isn't flawed by compensating moves.

In chapters 2 through 5, we'll take a look at you as a golfer. We'll cover the factors that influenced your past and current swing tendencies and patterns, apply some foundational concepts to position you for success, focus in on the key swing positions, and locate your dominant power source. In chapter 6 we'll move on to studying the best players on tour. I'm going to take you through the primary swings you see on tour and help you pick out the swing and player who fits you the closest; then you're going to further customize your swing around that particular tour pro swing model.

Then, in chapter 7, you're going to work toward becoming your own best coach and create your own *customized swing model*. The way you go about developing your swing is key, and I've developed a system for helping you do just that. The system includes determining the type of swing you have right now and how you developed it, your individual swing influences, and identifying areas for improvement and change based on your new understanding and analysis. Once these concepts are under your belt, you're going to start customizing your swing from the foundation up.

Most of the technique and drill descriptions in the book are written for a right-handed golfer. However, all of the information can easily be adjusted for the left-handed golfer by reversing the instructions.

Your Commitment

Now that we have the introductory information out of the way, it's time to get started with your golf lessons. During your first few lessons you'll be figuring out exactly how and why your swing developed the way it has. By the time you have worked your way through the book, you will be ready to begin practicing your fully customized, fundamentally sound, consistent, and repeatable swinging motion through the ball. Your new golf swing will have you swinging toward the target better than ever—and you'll be doing so more comfortably, with greater ease, and well within your physical parameters.

You must be willing to take the responsibility for your own improvement. You have to become your own best golf coach by managing the resources available to you. You can take heart in the fact that I'll be working alongside you every step of the way. I promise that whether you are thick or thin, male or female, strong or weak, flexible or stiff, old or young, tall or short, big or small (did I miss anybody?) that the assessment, instruction, practice drills, and playing knowledge you receive throughout this book will improve your golf swing and help *you* play better golf.

Finally, I welcome you to attend one of the programs at The Suttie Golf Academy. We offer winter programs in the south and summer programs in the north. You can find our locations on my Web site at www.JimSuttie.com.

Are you ready? Then let's move to the lesson tee.

A Mechanically Sound Swing

If you want to improve your golf swing, understand first that the image you have of your swing probably doesn't match your actual swing. Students sometimes argue with me about what's going on in their swings. For some, I videotape their swings and point out what they're doing, only to have them say, "But that's not how I swing!" In such cases I remind them that "feel is not real." Anyone who has ever watched his or her swing on video has seen the gap between the mental image of the swing and the real thing.

I once asked a PGA professional to execute a specific swing fundamental. He responded, "I can't do that. I'm a feel player." I explained to him that "feel" changes every day, whereas fundamentals and mechanics do not. The feel of your swing is not an accurate indicator of what's really occurring. In becoming your own best coach, don't rely on your perceptions during your swing. Use mirrors, videotape, and the comments of others with experience to help you understand what's occurring during your swing.

Are You Seeing What You're Feeling?

To help you match your perception to your actual swing, try this exercise. Simply follow the instructions and then answer the questions.

Equipment

You will need the following equipment:

- Camcorder
- Full-length mirror

Swing Check

Have someone record several of your swings. You'll probably need to watch the tape a few times to answer the following questions, taking notes for future reference, if necessary. (Note that some of the questions are phrased for right-handed golfers with wording for left-handers in parentheses.)

- Does your swing match your perception of your swing?
- Is your takeaway wide and extended or picked up?
- How is your posture?
- How is your alignment?
- Where is your ball? Forward or back?
- Is your backswing low and flat or high and upright?
- Are you turning your shoulders a complete 90 degrees?
- Are your legs stable during your backswing?
- Are your hands ahead of the clubhead at impact?
- Is your left (right) wrist flat and your right (left) wrist bent at impact?
- Is your right (left) heel in the air at impact?
- Is your head behind the ball at impact?
- Is your right (left) elbow into your right (left) hip at impact?
- Are your hips open at impact?
- Is your swing long or short?
- Can you hold your finish for 10 seconds?
- Are your knees touching at the finish?
- Are your hips facing the target?
- Is your chest facing left (right) of the target at the finish?
- Is your head positioned over your left (right) leg at the finish?

Insights

After viewing the tape, practice a few swings, checking your position in the mirror. This exercise can be eye opening; repeat it regularly to check if your swing really looks—and not just feels—like the swing in your head.

The Mind–Body Challenge

In addition to the unreliability of perceptions, the manner in which the brain and body work as a unit creates another unique challenge to changing your swing. Changing the golf swing is difficult because of the way we're wired. The nervous system is inclined toward repetition; it creates a pattern of every repetitive action, and it is these ingrained patterns that your body has been trained to perform. So, change can be difficult. In fact, when you're trying to change your golf swing, replacing old habits with new habits is likely the tallest hurdle you face. For this reason, in most golf lessons I focus my students' attention on incorporating only one change into their swing at a time. It takes time and repetition to transfer the aspects of a golf swing from short-term memory to long-term memory (and eventually to a subconscious level of the brain). The best way to go about it is to practice the new skill on a regular basis and be patient. Once one new skill has been ingrained, you can start working on changing another part of your swing.

When you're rewiring your brain through practice, make sure you heed your current limitations. You need to swing within the physical capabilities you have at the time—while also working to improve these capabilities. Sometimes the distance between where you are and where you want to be is quite large, but you can't skip steps and rush things. Just as runners can't progress from running 5 miles (8 kilometers) to 20 miles (32 kilometers) overnight, golfers can't expect to gain 100 yards (91 meters) on their drives after changing only a single aspect of their swing. Swing within your physical limits at the time, accepting that change occurs gradually rather than suddenly. No matter how long or straight your ball travels, it's always better (and healthier) to remain patient than to attempt to swing outside your limits. If you try to do too much too fast, you develop bad habits that will need to be broken later. An example of exceeding individual physical limits is a golfer who tends to be inflexible in the upper body trying to make a swing that is parallel to the ground at the top. The result is a lot of off-center, inconsistent shots. There is no one test to determine the limits of your physical ability, but it's a good bet that if your swing is wild and inconsistent, you are exceeding your physical limitations.

As you try to make improvements on a skill, don't overestimate your abilities. To do so is human nature, but try to guard against it. Don't try to be more powerful or flexible than you truly are. You'll only incorporate mechanics into your swing that have no business being there. Admiring Tiger Woods' fluid swing is one thing, but trying to duplicate his shoulder turn and extension through the ball is asking for a host of compensations that spell disaster (see figure 1.1). Very few golfers in the world have any business attempting to replicate Tiger's physical moves through the shot (though, as you'll see later, there are elements of Tiger's swing you *should* try if you fit the right physical profile). But you don't need to swing like Tiger, anyway—by maximizing your strengths and playing within your limitations you will make significant improvements in your game.

Some may note that even great players with great swings like Tiger's seem to search for their swings. For example, the last couple of years, Tiger has had trouble driving the ball consistently.

Tiger originally came out on the tour with a strong left hand grip and a shut position at the top of his swing. His swing came in on the takeaway and was slightly crossing the line at the top. His swing wasn't always perfect, but he could repeat it again and again. In particular, he was able to time his swing because of his stronger grip and less open clubface. Now, he is playing with a weaker left hand grip and is also trying to keep the club more in front of his body on the backswing and consciously rotate his left arm to open the face more at the top. Unfortunately, an open face and a laid-off position doesn't work well if you have fast leg action and fast hip rotation. This only makes Tiger's club get more inside out on the downswing. To offset this, he must then slow down his lower body rotation.

So, as you can see, even a great player like Tiger tries things that don't fit his natural physical abilities and his unique power source.

Figure 1.1 Tiger shows a great impact position with the hips open and the arms extended.

Defining the Ideal Golf Swing

To help you find your perfect swing, you need a standard of reference. I began my doctoral thesis with an attempt to discover which methods of teaching and learning produced the *best* golf swing for the majority of golfers. The first problem I ran into was attempting to define *the best golf swing*. Thankfully, golf is not like mathematics or physical sciences, which lend themselves to precise quantification. Discussing, teaching, researching, and learning the golf swing are complicated by the fact that golf clubs are swung by human beings, none of whom is the same as another (figure 1.2).

Figure 1.2 *(a)* Mark O'Meara, *(b)* Phil Mickelson, and *(c)* Corey Pavin all have distinctive swings. Two characteristics all great ball strikers have in common are a flat left wrist at impact and a bent right wrist (or a bent left wrist and flat right wrist, in Phil's case). Although all swings look different, it's the commonalities you should copy.

a

b

c

I began my research with a simple question: Who are the best golfers ever to play the game? My short list included the likes of Byron Nelson, Ben Hogan, Sam Snead, Bobby Jones, Gary Player, Arnold Palmer, and Jack Nicklaus. Then I asked myself, *does any one of these golfers have a perfect swing?* If so, how can I tell? Did a perfect swing depend on the average distance and accuracy of their drives, their number of tournament wins, the amount of money they won? Clearly not. All of these players were great ball strikers, and they all got the job done on the tour—but they all swung the club differently.

The more past and present professionals I looked at, the more painfully obvious it became that no single tour player, man or woman, could help me find the answer I was searching for. There were many subjective criteria I could have used, but I needed a swing model that was measurable and objective and that would hold up to statistical analysis. I finally realized that I needed to employ a computer model to help isolate and understand the ideal swing.

As you might expect, each of the swings I entered into the high-tech computer software program was unique. Some of the pros played the game with a fade, some played with a draw, and others hit the ball straight down the fairway. Most hit the ball fairly high, but a surprising number of them hit with a lower trajectory. Each of their ball flight patterns and swing patterns was different. The only part of their swings that looked about the same at first glance was their club-to-ball impact, but with further study even this aspect slightly differed for each player.

As a lover of the game of golf, I had thoroughly enjoyed my research, which involved close scrutiny of the swings of players I greatly admired. But in the end I had to admit that not one of the swings I had studied was *the* perfect swing, *the* best swing above all others. Conceding this, I decided to try for a composite—to take an average of the key elements of the swings of the game's best players to come up with the most mechanically sound swing model possible.

The Mechanically Sound Swing Model

Focusing on the full swing, I created a mathematical average of 25 pro swings (among the pros I used were Mark O'Meara, Jack Nicklaus, and Al Geiberger). Once the average was complete, some amazing discoveries emerged. I ended up with a composite swing in which all anatomical differences were averaged. All swing peculiarities, hitches, and idiosyncrasies disappeared. The computer model accepted only those elements that were similar in all swings and discarded the differences with precision. After all the calculations, a mechanically sound swing emerged that I believe all instructors and players can use as their primary model. I defined the swing as follows:

A mechanically sound golf swing delivers the clubface through the ball perfectly square to the target line, perfectly vertical, so that only the loft of the club affects the trajectory of the shot, on the correct path, with maximum velocity at the bottom of the swing arc every single time.

Finally, in adding this swing to my instructional arsenal, I could say with confidence that I could help amateur players swing the club and contact the ball the same way tour pros do it. My model's ball flight trajectory was average height and produced a straight shot with a very slight draw. Given the data from the model, I knew we could expect all mechanically sound swings to do the following:

- Deliver the clubface to the ball at impact in a position perfectly square to the target line, and along a swing path straight down the target line
- Keep the clubface absolutely vertical through impact so that only the loft of the club affected the trajectory of the shot
- Generate maximum clubhead velocity just past the bottom of the swing arc
- Contact the ball precisely in the middle, or sweet spot, of the club-face
- Be capable of being repeated the same way each and every time

As a golfer, if you are able to re-create the angle and path of the clubface as just described, no matter how else you swing your club, you will have an outstanding golf swing. Bobby Jones once said, "The only reason we bother with the form and the correct swing is to find the best way of consistently bringing about the proper conditions at impact."

The ideal golf swing can be defined as a side-of-the-line hitting game, because we are standing to the side of the ball. Because of the position of the ball there is an inward dimension in the swing and an up-and-down dimension in the swing. The body turn creates the inward motion and the hands and arms create the up-and-down motion. It is the synchronization of the body turn and the up-and-down motion of the arms and hands that allows us to make our best swing.

In addition to understanding the key characteristics of the mechanically sound swing, you should be aware of three other points:

1. There are *no* compensations in the swing.
2. The computer-generated golfer swinging the club turned out to fit an ideal body type.
3. The simulated golfer possessed ideal flexibility, strength, timing, tempo, and rhythm and was able to maintain balance through the entire swing.

The Mechanically Sound Swing Versus Your Swing

Whether you're a recreational or serious golfer, the mechanically sound swing gives you a point of reference from which to start and a standard to return to when your swing goes off track. The computer-simulated golfer (see figure 1.3, a and b) has no compensations or deviations from the bench-

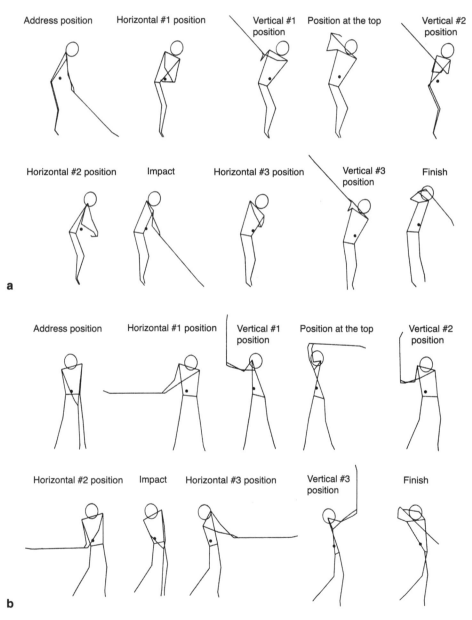

Figure 1.3 *(a)* Down-the-line and *(b)* side views of key positions in the mechanically sound golf swing.

marks established for the swing, so you can think of the swing as the ideal neutral swing. All golfers, even the pros, make compensations that deviate from this model swing. By understanding *why* you make compensations, and by avoiding or minimizing any unnecessary compensations, you can play as closely as possible to your own mechanically sound swing.

The first major swing difference between our simulated golfer and the typical golfer is physique. The computer-generated golfer is based on ideal attributes, including ideal body proportions, an ideal build, and ideal flexibility, as well as ideal strength, timing, tempo, rhythm, and balance through the golf swing.

The reality is that most of us in one way or another have to overcome physical challenges such as less-than-perfect height, weight, strength, or flexibility. Some of us have unusual physical attributes such as flat feet, high arches, one leg longer than the other, or chronic back pain. It's also unlikely that many of us are gifted with precise rhythm, timing, and balance. That's okay. One of the most important things this book can do for you is to help you choose the appropriate compensations to meet your own unique set of challenges. You *can* learn from the tour pros—but only if you know what you're looking for. Throughout this book I will point out deviations from the mechanically sound golf swing and explain the compensations that need to occur in many different kinds of golf swings, including yours.

Conceptualizing the mechanically sound swing model is the first step in your customization process. The next step is to determine where you are now in relation to the model. In chapter 2 we will analyze your present swing.

Your Present Swing

"How are you hitting it today?" is a time-honored question among golfers that is similar to asking someone, "How are you?" That is, the question doesn't usually request or receive a very detailed answer. But when I ask my students how they're hitting, I'm looking for quite a bit of detailed information. Specifically, I want to know the following:

- When you hit the ball consistently, where is it going?
- What is your worst shot?
- Do you miss the ball both ways or only in one direction?
- Are you missing only with certain clubs?
- Which club is your favorite? Which is your least favorite?
- Do you take divots? What do they look like?
- Where on the club do you feel the ball is hitting?
- Are you trying to draw the ball or fade the ball?

Once I get answers to these questions, I can determine where a golfer is with his or her swing and what needs to be corrected.

The first step to evaluating your swing is completing the Golf Swing Evaluation Sheet beginning on page 25. Completing the evaluation sheet will help you get the most out of this chapter. Complete as much of the information as you can at this point; you'll be returning to the Additional Information section often for reference and to add information.

Ball Flight

The first step in analyzing your swing is to take a look at your current ball flight—a direct indicator of how well you're swinging the club. Think of the ball flight pattern using only your driver and irons.

Typically, there are nine ball flight classifications: straight, straight push, straight pull, push slice, push hook, fade, draw, pull slice, and a pull hook or duck hook. See figure 2.1, a and b, to identify the current ball flight pattern of your drives. Figure 2.1, a and b, shows ball flight classifications for both right- and left-handed players.

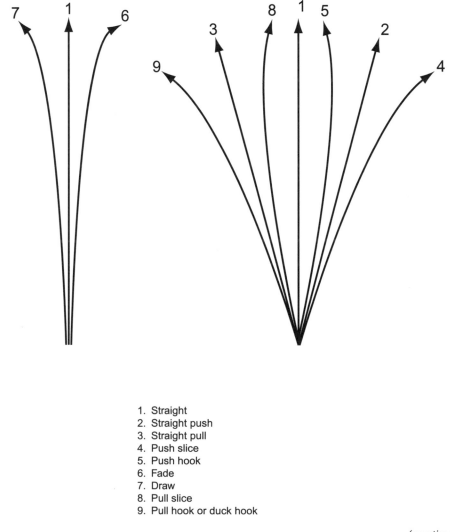

1. Straight
2. Straight push
3. Straight pull
4. Push slice
5. Push hook
6. Fade
7. Draw
8. Pull slice
9. Pull hook or duck hook

a

(continued)

Figure 2.1 Ball flight classifications for *(a)* right-handed players.

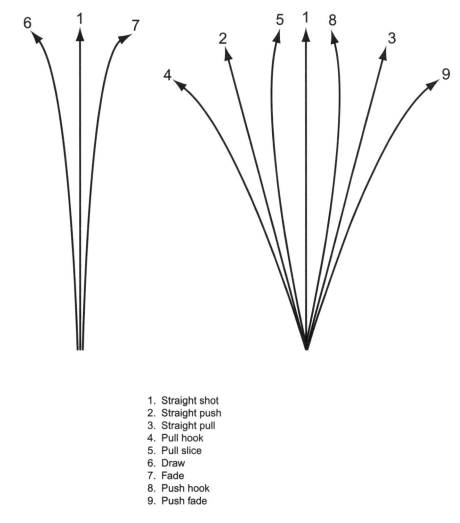

1. Straight shot
2. Straight push
3. Straight pull
4. Pull hook
5. Pull slice
6. Draw
7. Fade
8. Push hook
9. Push fade

b

Figure 2.1 Ball flight classifications for *(b)* left-handed players.

Face Angle and Swing Path

The laws of physics rule when it comes to producing ball flight. What matters most is the *face angle* of the club at impact. Figure 2.2, a through c, illustrates the three primary angles of the clubface at impact—open, square, and closed.

After the face angle, check your *swing path*. The direction and degree of the curve of the ball are directly related to how the face and the path interact at impact. Figure 2.3, a through c, illustrates the three primary swing paths of the clubhead at impact.

The relation of the face angle of your club and its path through impact play key roles in determining ball flight. Your shot slices or hooks in response

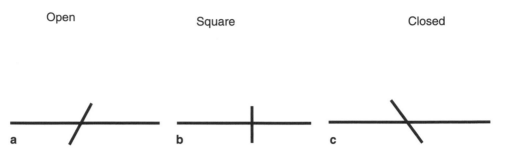

Figure 2.2   *(a)* open, *(b)* square, and *(c)* closed angle of clubface at impact.

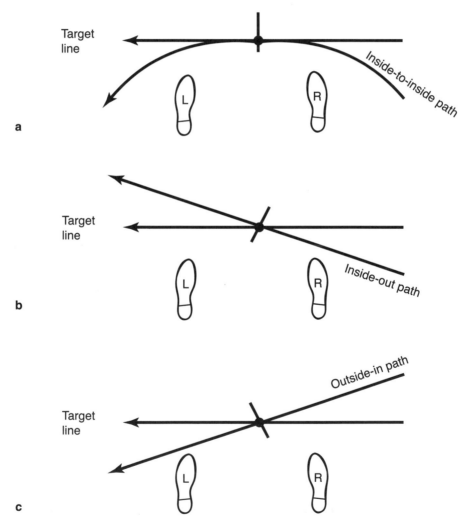

Figure 2.3   The three primary paths of the clubhead: *(a)* face square to path (straight shot), *(b)* face closed to path (hook), and *(c)* face closed to path (slice). Note: It is the interelation of the face and path that determines the ball's flight.

to the face of your club being either open or closed at impact. Golfers must understand the importance of face angle and swing path at impact or their shots will pay the price.

If the face is open at impact and the path is inside out, a push slice will occur. If the face is closed at impact and the path is inside out, the result will be a push hook. If the path is outside in and the face is open, the result will be a pull slice. If the path is outside in and the face is aimed left of the path, the result will be a pull hook or a duck hook.

The face has more to do with the direction of the shot than the path, but it is how face and path interact at impact that determines the shot you're hitting. If you want to return to the videotape you made in chapter 1, you might choose to revise some of your answers on the Golf Swing Evaluation Sheet based on your new understanding of face angle and path.

With any bad shot you hit, try to fix the face first, and the path will fall in line. For example, if a golfer comes to me with a slice, I will do anything I can to fix the clubface first. I might strengthen his or her grip or even turn the face in a little. Once the ball starts going to the left, you may be surprised to see the golfer start swinging out to the right without telling him or her to do so. This is a reactionary thing that almost every slicer will do. Remember, the clubface has the most influence on the ball's flight, so fix it first.

Let's look at the most important types of ball flight in detail: the straight shot, the draw, and the fade. Understanding these three flights will give you command of the majority of the shots you'll need on the course. If you're hitting on any of the other swing paths, the goal is to get back to one of these three.

Straight Shot

The following is general information about the straight shot:

- Shape of the shot: Dead straight
- Angle of clubface at impact: Square to the target line and square to the path
- Path of swing at impact: Straight down the target line
- Result: In reaction to the square clubface, the ball travels on a straight line and continues down the target line

Why don't we all simply cut out draws and fades and just hit the ball straight? The explanation is simple—although it's ideal to hit the ball straight to where you aim it each time, this shot pattern is the toughest pattern to pull off consistently. When you try to hit a straight shot, you don't eliminate one side of the fairway, which is a very important playing strategy. When you start missing your straight shots, balls might go either right *or* left of the fairway, which can quickly lead to trouble. A player who produces a predominantly straight ball flight must work very hard at limiting misses to one side of the fairway or the other. In contrast, if a player is hitting fades or draws, chances are much better of missing to only one side of the fairway, which significantly increases the likelihood of hitting the fairway on more shots. This is why you should build fade fundamentals or hook fundamentals into your swing.

Remember that when a ball begins to curve the curve is a function of the spin created by the angle of the clubface at impact. The ball's initial direction is determined by the clubface path through impact. The ideal path for a straight shot is from inside the target line on the downswing to straight down the line through impact and back inside the line on the follow-through (figure 2.4).

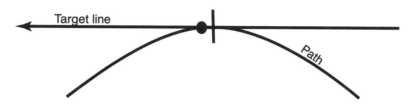

Figure 2.4 An inside-to-inside path. A shot will go straight when the face angle and the path are aimed in the same direction at impact.

Draw

The following is some general information about the draw:

- Shape of the shot: Starts out right and curves subtly to the left for right-handed golfers and subtly to the right for left-handed golfers
- Angle of clubface at impact: Slightly closed to the path
- Path of swing at impact: Inside out
- Result: Because of the inside-out swing path, the ball starts out to the right of the target, then draws gently because of a slightly closed club-face

A draw produces a tumbling, forward spin, similar to topspin in tennis. One advantage of this spin is the potential for more distance off the tee because the ball rolls forward after it lands. However, keep in mind that a draw hits greens with the same forward spin, often making for more roll than you want on approach shots. Also, with too much spin a draw can turn into an out-of-control hook that starts in one direction and curves dramatically to the left, losing both distance and direction (see figure 2.5). Once in a while you might want to hit an intentional hook to get out of trouble, but this shot shouldn't be part of a regular swing pattern.

Players who draw the ball also fly the ball a bit lower on average than golfers playing a fade. Lower ball flight tends to eliminate, or greatly reduce, the impact of wind on ball flight. Though a draw helps when hitting into the

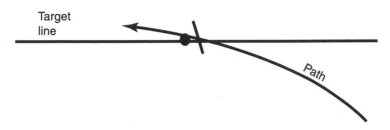

Figure 2.5 A shot will hook when the path of the clubhead is coming from inside the target line but the face of the club is aimed to the left of the path at impact.

wind, it is harder to take advantage of a big downwind gust the way you can when you fade the ball with a high ball flight. Golf is a game of tradeoffs, so pick your shots to match the circumstances of the situation.

Fade

The following is some general information about the fade. See figure 2.6 for an illustration of the fade.

- Shape of the shot: Starts out left and then curves subtly to the right for right-handed golfers and subtly to the left for left-handed golfers
- Angle of clubface at impact: Slightly open
- Path of swing at impact: Left of the target line at impact
- Result: Because of the left swing path, the ball starts out slightly left of the target, then fades gently because of a slightly open clubface

A fade starts out left of the target and then curves gently left to right for right-handed players and right to left for lefties. A slice is too much fade that starts curving right away, out of control, heading for the neighboring fairway. As with a hook, you can hit an intentional slice to get out of trouble, but that's a specialty shot, not a consistent shot pattern.

A fade has more backspin on it than a draw, with a higher ball flight. A lot of tour players prefer a fade because it allows them to aim directly at the pin because a high ball with backspin stops much quicker on the green. This comes in handy when the pins are tucked tight into the corners on Sunday.

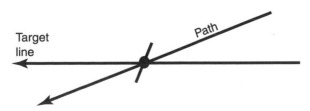

Figure 2.6 A ball will fade or even slice when the path of the club is coming from outside in through impact and the face is angled right of the path.

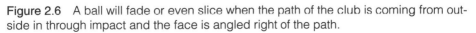

Other Ball Flight Patterns

To better understand the golf swing, you should understand the other six flight patterns as well—the straight pull, pull hook, pull slice, straight push, push slice, and push hook. If you're hitting any of these patterns consistently, practice changing your swing path and face angle until you're hitting a fade, straight shot, or draw. You might be amazed how much distance you can gain just by turning a hook into a draw or a slice into a fade. Slices and hooks use up valuable distance going in the wrong direction.

- **Straight Pull:** The straight pull travels on a straight line to the left because the swing path is going left and the clubface is square to the path. Flies straight right for lefties.
- **Pull Hook:** Starts out like a straight pull, then hooks even farther in that direction because of the closed clubface and outside-to-inside path of the clubface.
- **Pull Slice:** Starts out like a straight pull, then slices back in the other direction once airborne. Results from an outside-to-inside swing path and open clubface.
- **Straight Push:** Ball flight is straight right because the clubface path is inside-to-outside, with the face square to the path. Flies straight left for lefties.
- **Push Slice:** Starts out like a straight push, then slices even farther in that direction because the path is very inside-to-outside and the face angle is open to this path.
- **Push Hook:** Similar to the push slice, the ball starts out like a straight push because of the inside-to-outside path, but this time the ball hooks back in the opposite direction because the clubface is closed to that path at impact.

From these brief descriptions you can see that the pull, the pull hook, the pull slice, the straight push, the push slice, and the push hook are shots that golfers can rarely control and hit with consistency. These shots have such a large dispersion pattern that it's nearly impossible to play these shots as part of your game—your scores would soar.

Now that you have identified the primary ball flight pattern of your shot with a driver, work through the same process with a 5-iron. It's rare that I run across a golfer whose iron and wood swings are the same, including in the pros. Each swing tends to be different, and players always seem to be better with one or the other. This is due in part to ball position. Because you drive the ball from a teed position, your clubface hits the ball while traveling slightly on the upswing, so a sweeping path through the swing is more effective. In contrast, fairway shots must be executed with a descending blow to the ball to get it airborne. Thus, a descending rather than a sweeping path through the shot is more effective on the fairway.

Choosing a Draw Versus a Fade

Play a draw if . . .

- You want or need added distance on your shots.
- Most of the course layouts you play favor draws or are neutral (favoring neither draws nor fades).
- Target greens are larger or there are fewer greenside hazards.
- You often play in windy conditions and want to keep your ball flight lower.
- You enjoy and prefer this ball flight.

Play a fade if . . .

- You prefer a higher ball flight and need to stop the ball quickly on hard, fast greens.
- Distance is not a problem, but control is
- Most of the course layouts you play favor fades or are neutral (favoring neither draws nor fades).
- Target greens are smaller or there are many greenside hazards (especially water).
- You like to take aim at pins.
- You enjoy and prefer this ball flight.

For both types of shots consider where the hazards are on any given hole, because it's a big advantage to move the ball away from trouble. If the ball doesn't move as much as you thought, usually a straight ball will still be fine. An exception is if you have to start the ball out over a hazard and hope the shot draws or fades back to safety—this causes trouble if the ball doesn't move as much as you expected. Ben Hogan and Jack Nicklaus both chose to hit a fade because a draw is difficult to hit consistently and accurately.

If you hit either a fade or draw consistently, you shouldn't attempt to hit the opposite shot out on the course unless you have practiced and developed the shot ahead of time. Once you can hit the draw consistently enough to eliminate one side of the fairway, you can try adding a fade to your shot-making repertoire.

Now that you've identified your ball flight pattern, take a minute to look back and consider these questions: What ball flight would you prefer to work toward with your driver? What ball flight have you decided to work toward with your irons? What type of ball flight have you grown accustomed to?

Your expectation for the flight of your ball has a much greater influence on your game than you might imagine. You're probably not aware of it, but you have already learned to react to ball flight. On the other hand, your preferred ball flight could be an aesthetic taste of yours that has nothing to do with the practical side of the game. You might prefer to hit the ball high because you like that type of flight—it gives you more of a thrill. If so, consider sticking with that ball flight and work at becoming more consistent.

Did you produce a tremendous slice as a beginner? Most golfers do, and they've done everything they can think of, read about, or heard of to stop slicing. If you're still slicing, you're undoubtedly swinging from outside to inside the target line and cutting across the ball with an open clubface. To make matters worse, you aim farther and farther left of your actual target in an attempt to compensate for the slice. And what do you do as a result? You hit an even worse slice. The irony about slicing is that you see the ball going right on one shot and subconsciously start swinging more to the left on subsequent shots, which only makes your outside-to-inside swing pattern worse. See chapter 3 for more information about proper alignment.

As you analyze your swing, remember that the interaction of the face angle and the swing path at impact will produce your present shot pattern. Also note that of the two, face angle has the greatest impact on the outcome of the shot. Pay particular attention to the grip because that is how we gain control of the face angle.

Reading Your Divots, Clubface Marks, and Misses

The second step in analyzing your swing is to examine divots, clubface marks, and misses. Combined with the ball flight information, you'll have more tools to figure out why shots fly the way they do. You'll be able to figure out clues such as clubface angle (open or closed), path (outside in or inside out), and how you're transferring weight in your swing. And, more important, you'll have a better idea of what to fix to get your swing back on track.

Reading Divots

The size, direction, length, and depth of your divots can tell you volumes about your swing. Divots tell you the angle of approach and the path of the clubhead through impact. For example, divots that are deeper at the toe indicate either excessive hand action through impact or that the lie angle of your clubs is too flat. Divots that are too deep indicate excessive lunging or chopping in your downswing. If there's no divot, this tells you that you're a "picker" and not a "digger" and that you're probably hanging back on your back leg when you swing and are scooping with your right hand.

Here are some common kinds of divots and the information they reveal about your swing:

- Rectangular (ideal) divots: The best divot to have is a rectangle about the length of a dollar bill and the width of the clubface. When you see this divot, be satisfied because it means you're squaring the blade of the club through impact.

- Left-angled divots: If the divot angles to the left of the target line, you're swinging outside to inside. The path of your club is undoubtedly going left of your target, which typically produces a straight pull. If the blade is shut at impact, the ball hooks even more to the left, which is a pull hook. If the divot is square but angles to the right of your target, your swing path is going to the right, and a push or hook will result.

- Right-angled divots: If the divot curves to the right of the target, the path was inside out at impact, and you have pushed or hooked the ball. If the divot is deeper than usual, your swing is too steep or you might be using your hands too much through impact. You're driving the club farther down into the turf than necessary, thus dissipating energy into the ground rather than to the target. If you do manage to contact the ball first, the clubhead is not going to *pop* (accelerate) through impact, and you'll still lose distance. A swing path that's too steep will often cause fat shots, which lose all their energy by hitting the dirt before the ball. Toe-deep divots that are left of the target line mean the toe of the club is getting to impact first and you're probably using your hands too much through impact.

- Deep divots: Divots that are extremely deep, besides being a superintendent's nightmare, usually indicate a high swing that comes right on top of the ball. This means your upper body is getting ahead of the ball at impact and you have to throw your hands at the ball at the last second just to catch up.

- No divots: Not making any divot signals that you're not staying down through the shot. You lifted your body and came out of your posture, or you shortened your arms through impact. As another possibility, make sure that you're not releasing your wrists too early in the downswing and scooping at the ball. Scooping is a common error among casual golfers attempting to help the ball into the air. This scooping motion causes the club to hit behind the ball and doesn't allow it to release properly through impact. Also, if you take no divot you are most likely swinging too inside-outside.

Reading Clubface Marks

Reading the clubface can tell you how well your clubs are fitted by showing how the path of the clubhead travels through impact. Where is the major wear on your clubface—on the toe, back on the heel, or on the sweet spot? Where is the wear on the bottom of the club? Areas of wear can tell you a lot about the correctness of your clubs' lie angles. I'm a lot like an old tracker: I can learn a lot from the clues you leave behind—and so can you. Here are a few common marks I see and the meaning behind them:

- Ball marks on the toe of your driver: The toe of your club is getting to the impact point first. This indicates your swing is too high, most likely caused by a "handsy" casting action in your downswing. To correct this, you need more body action and less hand action through impact. This kind of ball mark could also mean that you could be cutting across the ball so much that only the toe hits the ball. You should also flatten your swing at the top and try to swing more on the inside track coming down.

- Ball marks on the heel of your driver: Your shoulders are dominating the downswing with an outside-in swing, or your swing could be on an extremely inside path so that the heel hits first. Either way your swing is usually too low.

- Tee marks on the bottom of your driver: Tee marks appear on the sole of your driver where paint from the tee is scraped off. If the line runs diagonally from the heel to the toe, you have cut across the ball from outside to inside the target line, caught the ball on the toe of the club, and produced a slice. If the tee mark is straight across the sole, from leading edge to the back, and in line with the sweet spot, you've probably hit the ball dead center. If the mark runs diagonally from toe to heel, you swung from too far inside the target line, caught the ball toward the heel of the club, and pushed it off to the right. As you can see, this clue tells you not only where you hit the ball on the clubface but indicates your swing path as well.

Reading Missed Shots

You'll notice on the Golf Swing Evaluation Sheet that I not only ask you where your hits go but also where your misses go and how frequently you think you miss shots. I also ask if there are one or two shots that you tend to miss more than others. This is valuable information for an instructor. When you're hitting shots out of bounds, it's my responsibility to stop those shots as quickly as possible.

The shot you fear the most must be removed from your mind in order to free your mind up to customize your swing. To find out exactly where the face of the club is striking the ball, buy some pressure-sensitive tape (available online or from many pro shops) that attaches directly to the clubface. This gives you hard and fast evidence of a black mark on the pressure-sensitive paper at the point which the ball made contact with the club. Each piece of paper has a circle in the middle that you position over the sweet spot of the clubface. Take several swings to find the most consistent impact pattern on the clubface. You can tell a lot from these impacts; anything above, below, left, or right of the sweet spot means you're not swinging the club on the ideal plane through impact and you're losing both distance and accuracy. Following are explanations of these impacts:

- Marks toward the heel of the club with a driver indicate your swing is too inside out through impact. Toward the heel on an iron means the lie angle is likely too upright for your swing.

- Marks toward the toe of the driver indicate the swing is too outside to inside across the ball. Using irons, it means the lie angle is probably too flat because the toe of the club is getting there first. If that's the case, impact will feel very tinny, and a poor shot results.

- Marks high on the clubface with the driver could mean one of two things: The angle of approach is too steep and choppy, or you're hanging back on the right side (left for lefties) at impact and casting or scooping underneath the ball. Your ball position is usually too far back in your stance. With irons, it means you're scooping or hitting up with the irons instead of striking a descending blow.

- Marks below the center of the face with a driver generally mean you're hitting up on the ball too much and the ball is too far forward in your stance. Hitting below center with irons produces a low ball flight, which means that the sweet spot has drifted forward (past the ball) and the angle of approach is too steep. This happens when the swing center gets past the ball at impact.

Steep and Narrow Swings Versus Shallow and Wide Swings

Generally speaking, a golf swing is either too high at the top and too steep coming down or too flat at the top and too wide coming down. For every swing I see too flat and too shallow, I see 10 swings that are too high and too steep.

Swings that are too high generally come down outside in. This is due to the early unwinding of the shoulder and torso from the top. The resulting shots are pulls, toe shots, pull slices, tops, slices, and shots that curve to the right. The correction for this is a lower swing plane at the top and less body action coming down. This creates a shallower, more inside approach to the ball. If you hit big divots that seem to go left of your target, you are too high at the top and too steep coming down. If this is you, do some baseball swings with your club, trying to get a feel for a flatter swing.

On the other hand, some of you may not get any divot with your irons. This usually means your swing is too flat and shallow, and inside out coming down. The shots you will tend to hit are hooks, pushes, thin shots, and fat shots. A lot of the marks on your clubface will be toward the heel. If this sounds like you, you will have to make your swing higher and use more body and less hands and arms coming down.

If you're better with your driver than you are with your irons, there's a good chance that you have a flat, wide, shallow, and inside-out swing. If you're good with your short irons and not so good with your longer clubs, there's a good chance you are like most of the golfing population: too upright, too steep and narrow coming down, and probably outside in through impact.

I hope this chapter has given you a good idea of where your swing is now as well as a solid understanding of the many factors that influence your swing. The next step is establishing or solidifying your swing foundation, which we'll work on in the next chapter. After that, we'll be able to slot you into categories based on your physical attributes and power source (chapter 5). But before moving on, I ask for your patience. Realize that old habits are difficult to build over, and ingrained swings are difficult to alter—but, you probably know this from years of frustration! To change your current swing, you need to recognize its strengths and weaknesses and understand how and why it developed as it has. This relearning process is like digging the weeds out of your front yard. If you cut just the tops off, they'll grow right back. We need to get to the root causes of your swing problems, but that's not going to happen in a short golf lesson. Finding your perfect swing is going to take some time. But stick with it—the journey is worth it, and you'll have fun along the way.

Golf Swing Evaluation Sheet

Sometimes we understand something better when we can write it down and analyze it, and this is also very true of golf swing tendencies. Answer the questions on the following pages as best you can, and this self-evaluation will give you a realistic and objective evaluation of your present swing.

Name: _____

Handicap: _____

Date: _____

Present ball flight problem (with your driver, irons, and short game):

_____

_____

_____

My worst club: _____

My best club: _____

Body type: ❏ Tall and thin   ❏ Short and stocky

            ❏ Average proportions   ❏ Other

Flexibility level: ❏ Very flexible   ❏ Somewhat flexible

                    ❏ Not very flexible   ❏ Very inflexible

Swing path: ❏ In to out   ❏ Out to in   ❏ Down the line   ❏ Don't know

Swing pattern: _____

Face angle: ❏ Square   ❏ Open   ❏ Closed   ❏ Varies

Divot size and depth (describe): _____

_____

Impact point: ❏ Center   ❏ Toe   ❏ Heel   ❏ Top   ❏ Bottom

Describe what you think are the major problems with your golf game:

_____

_____

_____

From *Your Perfect Swing* by Jim Suttie, 2006, Champaign, IL: Human Kinetics.

Describe the solutions you have tried to fix these problems:

_____

_____

_____

What solutions, if any, have been suggested to you but you have not tried?

_____

_____

_____

What drills or exercises have been suggested for improvement?

_____

_____

_____

What equipment has been suggested to be changed or added?

_____

_____

_____

Additional Information

After its initial path, the ball flight pattern of my drives is typically . . .

❏ Straight ❏ Draw ❏ Fade ❏ Straight pull ❏ Pull hook

❏ Pull slice ❏ Straight push ❏ Push hook ❏ Push slice

Comments: _____

With my driver, the initial flight is typically . . .

❏ To the right ❏ To the left ❏ Straight

My ball flight is . . .

❏ Consistent ❏ Inconsistent

The initial path of my irons is usually . . .

❏ To the right ❏ To the left ❏ Straight

From *Your Perfect Swing* by Jim Suttie, 2006, Champaign, IL: Human Kinetics.

After the initial path, the ball flight pattern of my iron shots is typically . . .

❏ Straight ❏ Draw ❏ Fade ❏ Straight pull ❏ Pull hook
❏ Pull slice ❏ Straight push ❏ Push hook ❏ Push slice

Comments: _____

My ball flight is . . .   ❏ Consistent   ❏ Inconsistent

I quite often hit . . .   ❏ "Fat" shots   ❏ "Thin" shots

My concept or definition of the golf swing is as follows:

_____

_____

_____

My role model out on tour is _____

because_____.

My favorite club when I took up the game was my _____

because _____.

My favorite club now is my _____

because _____.

I see my greatest strength in golf as _____.

My least favorite club now is my _____

because _____.

I see my greatest weakness in the game as _____.

The ball flight pattern I like the best is _____.

I am _____ years of age.

I have been playing golf for _____ years.

My current handicap is _____. The lowest my handicap has ever been is _____.

In season, I typically play or practice golf _____ times a month.

My typical golf season lasts from _____ to _____.

Most of my missed shots go _____.

From *Your Perfect Swing* by Jim Suttie, 2006, Champaign, IL: Human Kinetics.

My rating of the following factors (scale of 1 to 10):

Flexibility _____   Balance _____   Strength _____

Do I have any physical handicaps, injuries, or conditions that prohibit me from making a complete swing through the ball?   ❏ Yes   ❏ No

I typically take _____ golf lessons each season with . . .

❏ The same instructor   ❏ Different instructors from time to time

❏ Many different instructors

Comments: _____

Golf schools I have attended:

_____

I am looking to   ❏ Overhaul my golf swing   ❏ Fix a specific problem

❏ Other (please describe)

_____

I am willing to invest _____ hours a week to improve.

I am willing to invest in a series of golf lessons in order to improve: ❏ Yes   ❏ No

My short-term goals for my golf game:

_____

_____.

My long-term goals for my golf game:

_____

_____.

The best aspect of my game is my . . .   ❏ Driving ❏ Pitching

❏ Chipping ❏ Putting ❏ Iron shots ❏ Wood shots

The aspect that needs the most work is my . . .   ❏ Driving ❏ Pitching

❏ Chipping ❏ Putting ❏ Iron shots ❏ Wood shots

From *Your Perfect Swing* by Jim Suttie, 2006, Champaign, IL: Human Kinetics.

Other sports I have participated in, either now or in the past, include . . .

❑ Football   ❑ Baseball   ❑ Softball   ❑ Tennis   ❑ Hockey   ❑ Other

I am certain that my equipment fits me and my game.   ❑ True   ❑ False

My equipment was fitted by a professional.   ❑ True   ❑ False

Comments: _____

I have had my current equipment for _____ years.

Which statement best matches the environment you learned the game in?

❑ The courses I learned to play on were hilly and soft and gave up little roll.

❑ I learned the game in a place where the ground was usually flat and the wind was a constant factor.

❑ I learned the game in a place where the greens tended to be elevated and smaller in size.

❑ Other (please describe): _____

When I think about swinging the club, my thoughts are typically . . .

❑ Body thoughts   ❑ Clubhead or face thoughts   ❑ Shaft thoughts

❑ Target thoughts   ❑ Arms and hands thoughts   ❑ Pure emotion

❑ Ball flight   ❑ Pure feel   ❑ I have no idea what I am thinking about!

❑ Other (please explain) _____

I consider myself a . . .   ❑ "Feel" player   ❑ "Mechanical" player

More information on my divots and clubhead:

The size and shape of my divots tend to be:

_____

The direction of my divots is:

_____

The tee marks on my clubhead appear on the   ❑ toe   ❑ heel   ❑ center

Is the wear consistent on the sweet spot of my clubface?   ❑ Yes   ❑ No

From *Your Perfect Swing* by Jim Suttie, 2006, Champaign, IL: Human Kinetics.

I think my swing is...

☐ A body swing ☐ An arm swing

☐ A combination of arms and body ☐ A hands swing

The strongest part of my body is...

☐ My upper body ☐ My lower body

☐ My hands and arms ☐ I have balanced features

I hit my driver better than my irons. ☐ Yes ☐ No

I hit my irons better than my driver. ☐ Yes ☐ No

My worst clubs are...

☐ Short iron approaches ☐ 50 yards (about 46 meters) and in with wedges

☐ Fairway woods ☐ The driver ☐ Middle and long irons

☐ All of the above

I have...

☐ A low swing plane ☐ A high swing plane

My drive goes...

☐ Less than 200 yards (about 183 meters)

☐ 200 to 220 yards (about 183-201 meters)

☐ 220 to 240 yards (about 201-219 meters)

☐ 240 to 260 yards (about 219-238 meters)

☐ 260 yards (238 meters) or longer

I am...

☐ A fast, short swinger ☐ A long, slow swinger

From *Your Perfect Swing* by Jim Suttie, 2006, Champaign, IL: Human Kinetics.

Please provide any additional information you think might help improve your lessons:

_____

_____

_____

_____

_____

_____

_____

Use the following space for keeping track of information obtained during your golf lessons:

_____

_____

_____

_____

_____

_____

_____

_____

_____

_____

_____

_____

_____

_____

_____

_____

_____

From *Your Perfect Swing* by Jim Suttie, 2006, Champaign, IL: Human Kinetics.

A More Effective Swing

Now that you have a clear sense of your swing, the next step is to put your swing together. Building a swing is like building a house in that you start both tasks from the ground up. In creating your golf swing, you create the building blocks, the *fundamentals* common to all good golf swings. No matter what your swing tendencies, body type, or ball flight preferences, you need to develop a solid setup and alignment to serve as a point of reference to go to when your swing breaks down. Once you have the fundamentals in place, you can build and customize your perfect swing based on your body type, your personal preferences, and your pro swing model. So let's start our lesson here with a brief review of the mechanically sound swing and its fundamentals.

The Mechanically Sound Swing

You'll recall from chapter 1 that your primary goal in perfecting your golf swing is to deliver the clubhead to the ball *perfectly square* to the target line, *perfectly vertical* so that only the loft of the club affects the trajectory of the shot, with *maximum velocity* at the bottom of the swing arc, and in a *repeatable* fashion. Keep this goal in mind as you work through all of our lessons.

Building a mechanically sound swing involves three steps: perfecting your preswing (including your setup and alignment), which we cover in this chapter; mastering the key swing positions (chapter 4); and determining your primary physical power source (chapter 5).

Let's begin with developing your preswing position, which involves five components:

- The setup
- Alignment of the feet, knees, hips, shoulders, and eyes in relation to the target line
- Aiming the clubface on the target line
- Muscular readiness (relaxing the body, especially the hands and arms)
- Mental readiness

Your goal for this chapter is to make your setup position automatic. You should be able to repeat your setup consistently and automatically so that you no longer have to think about it. Once you can do this, you can devote your full attention to perfecting your swing position (discussed in the next chapter).

Setup

Working toward a mechanically sound swing during all elements of your swing, including the setup, is your goal and will give you a basis for comparison. When first working on your setup, focus on the *similarities* in your setup to those of the mechanically sound setup rather than on the differences. Bring the similarities in line first, and this should make it easier to work on the aspects of your setup that deviate most from the mechanically sound setup.

The importance of an athletic, tension-free, and balanced setup cannot be overstated. About 80 percent of all swing errors can be traced directly to errors and compensations in the setup or the takeaway (discussed in chapter 4). There's a lot to cover in the setup, but everything else hinges on it, so take the time to go through this chapter carefully.

An athletic setup depends on the following components: grip, posture, spine tilt, stance, arm position, ball position, and distance from the ball. I use the terms *athletic, active,* or even *animated* in my description of a sound setup, but this does not mean you move around a lot as you're addressing the ball. You should feel poised and ready to start the motion of your swing. Chi Chi Rodriguez compared his state of readiness during the setup to a jungle cat preparing to leap at his prey: poised to spring and hungry without being tense. You too must be poised in your lower body, ready to spring, and without tension. Here's an exercise to help you recognize the feeling you want to have during your setup readiness: Visualize yourself standing at the edge of a swimming pool. It's a hot day, and you can feel the heat. The water is inviting, and you're ready to jump in the pool feet first to cool off. Hook your toes over the edge of the pool. Bend your knees slightly. Bend forward slightly at the hip. Are you ready to jump?

As you stand at the pool's edge, you should feel focused but relaxed. This is the feeling of being *poised,* and it's this feeling you want to re-create each time you take to the green to prepare. Now let's move to your grip.

Grips

Your hands are the only parts of your body that transfer power directly to the club, so a proper grip is critical to the setup. Grips are classified as neutral, strong, or weak. The best grips share the following traits:

- They assist your hands in working as a single unit.
- They return the clubface square to the target line through impact.
- They keep the clubface perfectly vertical through impact.
- They transfer the greatest amount of energy from the swing, through the hands, and to the clubface.
- They allow the wrists to cock and release naturally and allow centrifugal force to work.

You cannot develop a good swing without a good grip—with a poor grip, you will not be able to square the clubface without making a lot of compensations in your swing. The grip is important because it is the only connection of your body to the clubface. The grip controls the clubface more than any other part of your body. How you hold the club will determine how your body will move. I base all of my teaching on what the face is doing during the swing and at impact, so the grip now becomes the most important fundamental that controls impact and the ball's flight.

In my initial research with the model swing, I didn't look at the influence of the grip on the swing, which was an oversight. I assumed that all grips were neutral, which is not the case. Grips are all a little different based on the size of the golfer's hands, hand strength, and flexibility, as well as the golfer's preferred ball flight. That being said, you now know why some unusual looking grips work well for some players. For example, Paul Azinger and Ed Fiori have strong grips. They have adapted their swings to fit their grips. In Paul's case, he has a hook grip and he neutralizes his grip during his swing by putting in fade fundamentals. Corey Pavin is another example of a golfer with a weak grip who puts hook fundamentals in his swing to neutralize the weak grip.

All grips, like all swings, are not the same. Most players adapt their body movement to fit their grip type. But, for the purposes of this book, we will refer to the neutral grip as the one to use to develop a neutral swing.

Neutral Grip

We'll discuss the neutral grip before strong or weak grips because the neutral grip, though not the most common grip, is the most natural and mechanically sound. In fact, the term "neutral," for our purposes, means mechanically sound. Thus, in subsequent sections, when you see the term "neutral," such as in "the grip is slightly stronger than neutral" or "the stance is open, closed, or neutral," the term *neutral* is referring to what occurs in a mechanically sound swing. The neutral grip is the perfect grip to use unless you need to compensate for another less-than-perfect aspect of your swing, game, or situation. For instance, players who are less physically strong than most others often opt to use a strong grip because it helps compensate for their lack of physical strength. We'll discuss this further when we cover strong grips in the next section.

A neutral grip fits neutral arm and hand action and neutral body action. For example, Robert Allenby, Stuart Appleby, and Al Geiberger use neutral grips to be able to work the ball either way. They tend to be shot makers, using their body equally with their hands and arms. In general, neutral grippers tend to be more interested in accuracy than distance. All aspects of their swings are balanced because of this grip type. By allowing gravity and centrifugal force to be the primary influences on the clubface angle through impact, golfers who use a neutral grip position allow the wrists to work properly through the entire motion of the swing. As we've mentioned, the term "neutral" means that the grip introduces no outside forces or compensations into the swing. Rather, energy flows naturally through the swing to the clubhead. There are several ways to ensure you have a neutral grip:

1. To get a good grip with the left hand, hold the club at a 45-degree angle with your right hand and then take your grip with your left (see figure 3.1).

Figure 3.1   Getting a good left-hand neutral grip.

2. You create a neutral grip for the right hand by simply "shaking hands" with your club (see figure 3.2a). When using a neutral grip, if you look at the back angle of the grip, you should see that the index finger of your right hand looks like the trigger finger when putting your hand on a gun (see figure 3.2b).

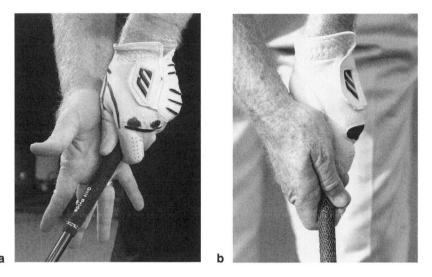

a   b

Figure 3.2 Neutral grip. *(a)* Shaking hands with the club. *(b)* Index finger of right hand like trigger finger.

3. To ensure you have a neutral grip and are standing the correct distance from the ball, stand with your arms hanging vertically down from your shoulder sockets with your palms facing (see figure 3.3) and then grip the club.

Figure 3.3 The palms-facing position ensures you have a neutral grip.

4. Stand erect with your arms at your sides—you'll notice that your arms will hang inward or outward depending on the roundness of your shoulders (see figure 3.4). To achieve a neutral grip, simply put your hands on the club the way your arms hang.

To get a feel for the neutral grip, try the following exercise with a partner. Stand straight with arms relaxed and elbows at your sides. Using the neutral grip as described (shaking hands with the club), hold a club in front of you and at the center of your body, parallel to the ground and with the clubface square. Ask your partner to hold the clubhead firmly. Now, lean back until your arms straighten (figure 3.5). Your partner should support your body weight as you lean

Figure 3.4 Stand with your arms at your sides to determine which way your arms hang (mine hang inward) and then grip the club that same way.

Figure 3.5 Neutral grip exercise.

back, straightening your arms and wrist. If your grip is truly neutral, the clubface will remain square. If the clubface turns to the left (closed), your grip is too strong. If the clubface turns to the right (open), your grip is too weak. (Thanks to Manuel de la Torre, a great teaching professional from Milwaukee, Wisconsin, for teaching me this exercise.)

Strong Grip

A strong grip positions the hands to maximize body swing rather than hand and arm swing. You'll want to keep this in mind in later chapters when we cover types of swings—your grip can work either with or against your body swing. A strong grip generally causes the clubface to shut during the swing, inhibiting hand and arm action and promoting a hooking (right to left) ball flight. Many PGA Tour players prefer strong left-hand grips. Golfers such as Paul Azinger, David Duval, and Lee Trevino like this grip because it facilitates a body swing and creates a more pronounced backswing turn and body rotation on the forward swing than a weak or neutral grip does. The strong left-hand grip works well for the slicer and for golfers with weaker, smaller hands because it helps hook the ball and increases power by encouraging the body to work. Most LPGA players choose to play with a strong left-hand grip because it gives them more power.

I recommend the strong grip to the average amateur or to players with less physical strength than average because this grip not only helps draw the ball but also creates speed through impact and makes for an inside-out downswing. A trend on the PGA Tour is to use a stronger than neutral grip and countering the effects of the grip with quick body action and hip turning through impact in order to hit a fade. This is an advanced way to use the grip, allowing players to avoid hooking the ball and to add distance to their fade shots. For the average player, a strong grip is a good measure to use to counter a slice.

In the strong left-hand grip, the right hand should mirror the left hand (figure 3.6). The palms face each other, with the club resting in the first joint of the right index finger. Be careful not to hold the club too much in the palm of the right hand. This is a common mistake that inhibits wrist and finger action and

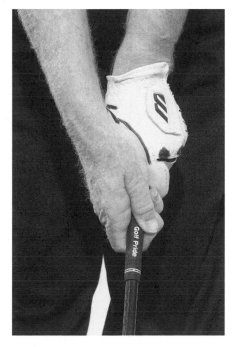

Figure 3.6 Strong grip.

slows club speed. Essentially, the right hand should use a finger grip and be positioned as described here:

- The lifeline of the right hand should be placed on top of the left thumb (see figure 3.7a).
- The little finger of the right hand should overlap or interlock with the index finger of the left hand.
- The club should be held in the first joints of the right hand (see figure 3.7b).
- The index finger of the right hand should trigger the clubshaft so that the V lines up with the left hand.

The following sections describe two drills to practice the strong left-hand and right-hand grip.

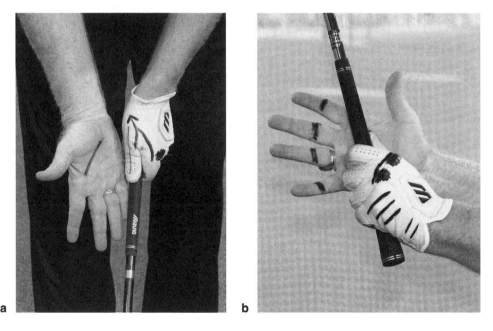

Figure 3.7 Right-hand position in strong grip. *(a)* Lifeline of right hand placed on top of left thumb; *(b)* the club rests in first joints of right hand.

Left-Hand Strong Grip Drill It's important for you to physically experience what I've been talking about in terms of the strength, neutrality, and weaknesses of grip positions. First, relax your hands and allow them to fall to your sides. When your hands and arms are relaxed, you should be able to feel the blood rushing to your fingertips. Pay attention to the force of gravity on your hands and fingertips as they dangle at your sides. Now pull the fingers of your left hand up and into the palm of the hand.

For most people, this move positions the left hand in a perfect, or nearly perfect, neutral grip. (Check a mirror to see what this looks like.) Now take your grip with the club to the side of your left leg (see figure 3.8), get into your stance, and set a 5-iron against the outside of your left leg. Allow your left arm to hang from its shoulder socket in a vertical position. Keeping your left hand relaxed and still hanging from your shoulder, place this hand on the handle of the club. Using a very relaxed motion, simply fold your left hand around the grip of the club. When you look at your hands, you should see only the two knuckles on the back of your left hand, as shown in figure 3.9.

Gently swing your left hand up, over, and into a position directly in front of your body, so that the 5-iron is perpendicular to your body. Make sure there's a slight *cup* in the back of your wrist. If you have completed the drill correctly, you will have produced a natural grip position for your left hand. Take a look at your grip and compare it to the one shown in figure 3.10. Does your grip match up?

Figure 3.8 Take your grip with your left hand to the side of your left leg.

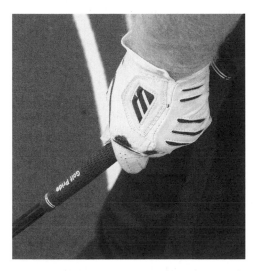

Figure 3.9 The neutral grip on the club. When you look down, you should see only the two knuckles on the back of your left hand.

Figure 3.10 The correct left-hand grip position in front of the body.

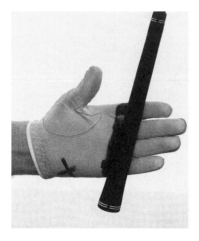

Figure 3.11 The handle of the club rests diagonally across the palm and into the first joint of the index finger.

Figure 3.12 The neutral left thumb. The crease between the thumb and index finger should point toward your right shoulder. Also notice the cup in the left wrist.

This is your left hand's neutral grip on the club. Now, with the 5-iron still in front of you, and as you look down at the back of your left hand and the face of the club, think of the back of your left hand as *being* the face of the club. That's right—think of the back of your left hand and the face of the club as being one and the same. Whatever the back of the left hand does in the swing, the clubface will do the same.

In the left-hand strong grip, your left hand is a combination palm and finger grip. The handle of the club rests diagonally across your palm and into the first joint (or root) of your index finger, as shown in figure 3.11. If you grip the club too far into the fingers, you'll get "wristy" and hook all day. If the club is too much in the palm, you won't use your wrists at all and will hit nothing but slices.

As you support the club in this fashion, the heel pad of your left hand is resting on top of the handle. Stop and take a full 30 seconds in this position, paying attention to the feel of your hand on the handle. It is more of a palm feeling than a finger feeling. This is your neutral grip that allows your left wrist to cock and release properly through the swing.

Now look at the back angle of your grip again; note that your index finger is slightly separated from your middle finger to allow space for the pinkie finger of your right hand. This overlapping grip is what you want at this point. You can work into a 10-finger or interlocking grip later if you find it works better for you, but for now go with the overlapping grip.

Now, with your left hand and golf club still positioned in front of you, look at the front angle of your left hand. Notice that the crease between the thumb and index finger points up toward your right shoulder, as shown in figure 3.12. If it doesn't, move it into the correct position. The left thumb should *not* extend down the shaft or be pulled up toward the top of the shaft. A "long" thumb creates a long swing and positions the club too much in the palm of the left hand (although experienced golfers sometimes use a long thumb to correct excessive "wristiness" through the impact area). On the other hand, an excessive "short" thumb creates a shorter swing and tends to overemphasize the wrist through the impact area. What you are seeing, or should be seeing, is a *neutral* left thumb. The thumb falls slightly to the right of the top of the handle, at about the 1 o'clock position on a clock (see figure 3.12). This positioning is important because it allows the left thumb to fit into the lifeline of the right hand and remain behind the shaft at impact.

If it sounds as if I'm devoting a lot of attention to the left hand and its role in the grip, it's because I am. The back of the left hand is the primary control for aiming the clubface. Taking the time to get your positioning right will pay off many times over as you improve your swing.

Right-Hand Strong Grip Drill As mentioned earlier, the right hand of an overlapping grip is more in the fingers than the left hand is. The handle of the club rests on the first knuckle of the right hand and runs diagonally through the second joint of the middle two fingers.

In the overlapping grip, the thumb of your left hand fits snugly into the crease of the lifeline of the right hand. This crease on top of the left thumb is one of three primary pressure points in the grip. The other two are the last three fingers of the left hand and the forefinger and thumb of the right hand. Try to be conscious of the amount of pressure you have in this type of grip. Generally speaking, fast swingers, such as Nick Price, hold the club a little tighter, whereas slower swingers grip the club more lightly. Normally, I advise against holding the club too tightly. In any case, grip pressure should be the same in both hands. Notice that the back of the right wrist is fairly flat and relaxed, whereas the back of the left wrist retains its cupped angle, as shown in figure 3.13. At impact this process is reversed: The back of the left wrist will be flat and the right wrist will be bent (see figure 3.14).

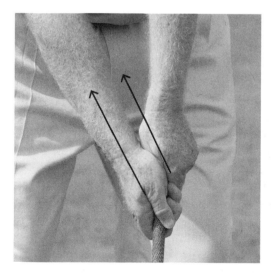 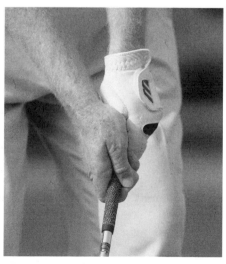

Figure 3.13 In the overlapping grip, the right wrist should be fairly flat and relaxed at address; the left wrist retains a cupped angle. Also, notice that the two creases are parallel.

Figure 3.14 At impact, the left wrist is flat and the right wrist is bent.

Look again at your hands, the crease (or V) formed by your thumb and index finger is parallel to the crease in the left hand. The thumb and index finger attach to a small muscle group that connects to the inside of your arm. If these fingers get too tight, the right side of your body dominates the motion. The muscles that attach to the last three fingers of the left hand are larger and should control the motion.

The two creases need to be parallel (see figure 3.13) because this ensures that the palms are facing one another in a *palms-facing* neutral grip. If the palms of the two hands are not facing, the wrists will not cock and release properly, and compensations will have to be made when gravity takes over near the bottom of the swing arc. Even if the grip is in a weaker position than neutral (or stronger than neutral), the palms should remain parallel.

Now, to get a feel of this parallel grip position, hold a club in front of you as previously described. Note the feeling of having both palms against the club in a parallel position to one another. Now rotate your hands to the right. This is a stronger grip position. Now return to neutral and rotate your hands to the left. This is a weaker grip position.

In an effort to feel more powerful and in more control of the golf club, some players torque their grip before they take the club back in what is known as a *dish-rag grip*. These golfers place both hands on the club in a fairly neutral position, but before taking the club back, they twist their hands in opposite directions, as you would rinse a dish rag. The left hand typically turns to the right, and the right hand turns to the left, causing the palms to move out of parallel position. In general, this is *not* the way you want to grip the club. The dish-rag grip typically causes the clubface to open and creates excessive right hand in the swing, resulting in a slice.

Overlapping, Interlocking, and 10-Finger Grips

In addition to the position of the hands on the club, it is also important to keep the hands working together as a unit during the swing. The overlapping, interlocking, or 10-finger grips serve this purpose. When using these grips, it is especially important to make sure that the knuckles of both hands line up. You also need to attend to how your hands connect on the club. With the overlapping grip (figure 3.15), your connection is cemented by the pinkie finger of the right hand resting on top of the index finger of the left hand (or sometimes in the space between the middle and index fingers of the left hand). The overlapping grip is one of the most popular among golfers.

For some golfers, an overlapping grip position is not the best fit. For instance, I recommend that most women, men with small hands, and players with below average hand strength consider either an interlocking or 10-finger grip (see figures 3.16 and 3.17), both of which add strength and control. With these two grip styles the wrists function a little more efficiently, which allows players with less strength to get more distance on the ball. The interlocking grip has the advantage of keeping the hands knit closely together through the entire swing. Tiger Woods and Jack Nicklaus use the interlocking grip, which they claim allows the hands to work together better.

For stronger players and players with large hands, I recommend an overlapping grip because it minimizes the role the hands play in the swing and typically helps create a more consistent shot pattern. Remember that the hands are basically two separate units that must come together as one unit in the golf swing. For this reason, I believe it's important to place them as closely as possible to one another. This can be achieved with any of the three grip styles, but if you use the 10 finger grip, you need to ensure that there's no separation between the hands. This is especially true at the top of the swing.

Figure 3.15 The overlapping grip with the knuckles lined up.

Figure 3.16 The interlocking grip with the knuckles lined up.

Figure 3.17 The 10-finger grip with the knuckles lined up.

Weak Grip

Very few players on the PGA Tour use weak grips. In my lessons, I rarely put an average golfer into a weak grip. However, at times a weaker grip best suits a player. For example, stand erect with your arms at your sides. If your hands hang outward because of a very straight back, then I might encourage you to try a weak grip. This would depend on the size and strength of your hands because the golfer who holds the club in a weak position (see figure 3.18) is a very hand- and arm-dominant golfer. These golfers depend on the rotation of the hands, arms, and forearms through impact to square the clubface. They are the exact opposite of a strong gripper, who depends on the body turn and passive hands for power. The weak gripper generally has a lot of hand and arm action on the backswing and plays with an open

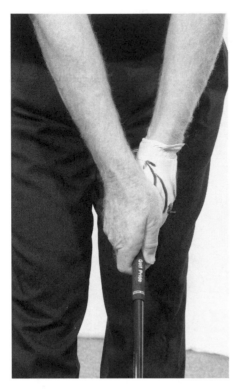

Figure 3.18 Weak grip.

face. To close the face, he or she must use a lot of hand and arm action on the downswing. The weak grip also tends to cause slicing and hook swings. The tradeoff is that these players can work the ball from either left or right and tend to be adept shot makers.

Unfortunately, it's difficult for the weak gripper to ever achieve distance because his grip stops him from using his body. Most average golfers are better suited to a strong grip to produce a hooking action and distance.

Wrist Action and Grip Pressure

In addition to the grip concepts we've covered so far, there are a few grip-related terms we'll come back to often, so it's important to understand them here. As mentioned earlier, a neutral grip position allows the energy of the swing to flow through to the club and creates an effective lever angle in the swing. Power in the swing is transmitted through to the hands and club-head. So, if the grip is incorrect, the wrists can't cock and hinge as they're supposed to during the backswing.

Wrist Action   As you grip a club and waggle the head back and forth, your wrists are *hinging*. If you reverse the directions of the clubhead, moving the clubhead up and down, your wrists are *cocking* and releasing. A sound grip allows both of these movements to happen naturally. One of the levers in your swing is the cocking action of your wrists on the backswing and the release of your wrists through impact. I suggest that you take a minute and duplicate the two movements so you can feel the difference in your hands, wrists, and forearms. Pay close attention to your wrist action in both hinging and cocking and to the difference in feel and range of motion (see figure 3.19, a-b).

In your swing, your right wrist both cocks and hinges on the backswing. If your grip is excessively strong or weak, it stops this natural motion. For example, if your hands are placed on the club in a position that's too weak (to the left for a right-handed player), the face will roll open (or pronate) on the backswing. Or, if the right hand is placed on the club too strong (too far to the right for a right-handed player), the right wrist can't hinge or cock properly on the backswing.

An exercise that helps you feel the range of motion in the wrist joint while ensuring your grip is neutral is called "cocking up." Simply take your grip with the club solidly on the ground. Without moving your shoulders or arms, cock your wrist up from the ground. If your grip is too strong or too weak, you'll be unable to cock the club very far off the ground.

An easy way to perform the correct wrist action is to think of the left wrist bent or cupped at address and the right wrist flat. As you go into your backswing, the left wrist flattens, and the right wrist bends. At the top of the swing, the left wrist is flat and cocked, and the right wrist is bent. As the downswing proceeds, just keep the left wrist flat and the right wrist bent all the way up to and through impact (see figure 3.20, a-b).

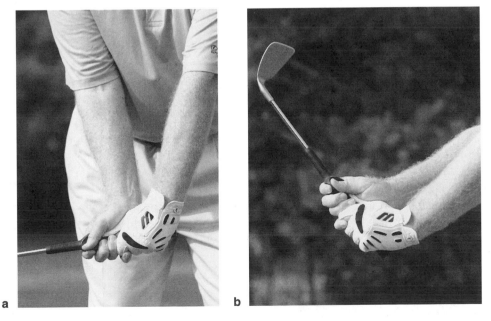

a   b

Figure 3.19 *(a)* Hinging the wrists. *(b)* Cocking the wrists.

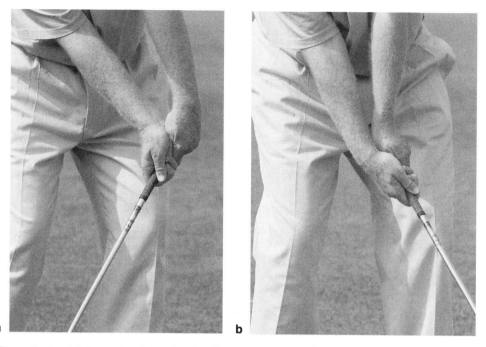

Figure 3.20 *(a)* Correct wrist action leading up to impact; *(b)* incorrect wrist action, with an early release, which results in scooping the ball.

As I've said, the wrists both cock and hinge when the grip is neutral. The right elbow is also a hinge joint and should be allowed to fold upward naturally in the backswing. If the grip is too weak, then the right elbow won't fold properly on the backswing. On the other hand, if the grip is too strong, the right elbow bends backward instead of folding upward, which causes the right elbow to get behind the golfer, creating all kinds of downswing problems.

Here are two drills to feel the proper movement of your right elbow. First, assume your usual golf posture with the club in front of you, but hold it only with your right hand. Maintaining your posture, fold your right arm 90 degrees and bring it up in front of you (see figure 3.21a). Just turn your body to the right on the backswing, keeping your right elbow bent 90 degrees and in front of your chest (see figure 3.21b). Now, swing down and extend your right arm in front of your body.

For the second drill, use two clubs. In your left hand, take the longest club in your bag and hold the clubhead end of your driver across your chest with your right arm over the top of the extended shaft. Make sure to keep the left hand connection to the left side of your chest as you do this exercise. Your left elbow should be pointing out at the target. Hold a short iron in your right hand as you address the ball (see figure 3.22a). Now, simply turn back, keeping the shaft on the left side of your chest and underneath your right arm (see figure 3.22b). This drill stops the right arm from getting behind the body on the backswing.

a

b

Figure 3.21   *(a-b)* Right elbow drill #1.

a

b

Figure 3.22   *(a-b)* Right elbow drill #2.

Generally speaking, the wrists and elbows cock and fold to 90 degrees at the top. Some swing styles are less than this, and some are more, but this is the average. One of your main power sources will be the cocking and hinging of your wrists and the folding and straightening of your right arm at the elbow. Without the correct grip, none of this can occur.

Grip Pressure   Finally, all grips exert a certain amount of pressure on the handle of the club. Working with hundreds of golfers has convinced me that grip pressure must be neutral. Most golfers find that on a scale of 1 to 10, with 10 being the most pressure, effective grip pressure doesn't fall below 3 and doesn't increase above 7. Within the range of 3 to 5, you're in pretty good shape, as long as the pressure remains constant throughout the swing. Too much pressure doesn't allow the wrists to function properly, and too little pressure causes a lack of firmness at the top of the backswing. As you swing a golf club, it should be obvious to you that the pull of centrifugal force automatically increases your grip pressure as the club moves toward the bottom of the swing. There must be a natural adjustment in the pressure of your grip—it can't be forced. As a reminder, it's easy to exert grip pressure with the wrong parts of the hands. The correct pressure points (for right-handed golfers) are

- the last two fingers of the left hand,
- on the lifeline of the right hand against the left thumb, and
- the right forefinger and the right thumb.

Now, get your 5-iron again, work through the grip pressure as previously described, and pay particular attention to the feel the club creates in your hands. This is what you're working to duplicate in your swing—the *feel* of the ideal grip position and pressure. I've noticed through the years that most high handicappers wear out their golf gloves in the heel pad of the left hand, which means the club is being held too much in the palm. Check your glove and see where the wear is. Also, this could be a sign of letting go of the club at the top. Also, if you cast the club from the top, it's a good bet that your grip is separating or coming apart at the top of your swing.

Grip Drills

Keep in mind that the tackiness of your club handles (grips) must be sufficient to help lock the club into your hands. When you feel as if you have to grip the club tightly to hold on to it through the swing, it's time to have your handles replaced. Here are several quick drills to check if your grip pressure is appropriate:

- Two-finger drill for grip pressure—Hold the club with only the index finger and thumb of your right hand (see figure 3.23). Support the club underneath the heel pad of each hand. Hit balls on a tee to feel the lightness in the hands and wrists.

- Claw drill—Put the index finger and middle finger of your right hand on the club, as shown in figure 3.24. Hit several balls. This drill takes excessive right hand and casting motion out of most swings, which cause the club to be released early, creating a scooping motion at the bottom of the swing.
- Double overlap drill—Overlap the entire right hand on top of the left, as shown in figure 3.25. This takes the right hand pushing dominance out of the downswing.

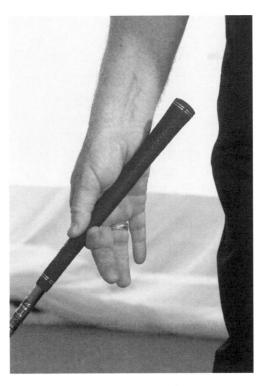

Figure 3.23 Two-finger drill.

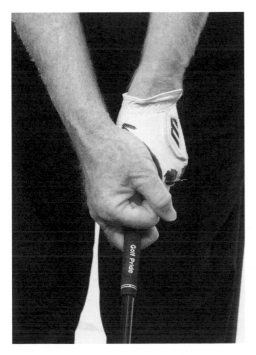

Figure 3.24 Claw drill.

Figure 3.25 Double overlap drill.

Figure 3.26   Right hand off at impact drill.

- Right hand off at impact drill—Hit several teed balls, taking the right hand off at impact, as shown in figure 3.26. This drill stops you from grabbing the club with your right hand at impact.

- Towel drill—Put a towel around a grip and hit several balls (see figure 3.27). By putting a towel on your grip, you'll naturally hold the club lighter.

- Right hand only drill—To get the correct motion and the correct pressure of the right side, swing a club with your right hand and arm only, as shown in figure 3.28.

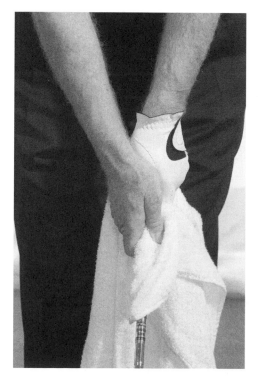

Figure 3.27   Towel drill.

Figure 3.28   Right hand only drill.

Posture

Posture can be defined as the angle of the knees, hips, and spine at address. Although each player's posture looks a little different, there's a balance point in every golf setup, and you must find yours. One objective of correct posture is to help you find, and maintain, your own balance point through the swing. Balance is so important in the setup that I have my students work through their setups on a balance board (see figure 3.29).

The idea is to get into your setup so that the board is balanced over the small beam running under it. I'd say 99 percent of my students have difficulty on the board the first few times, but they all get better because the board is a great teacher. As I mentioned, everyone's posture and balance point in the setup differs slightly because of different body builds and centers of gravity. The important thing is to find your balance point, develop an internal feel for it, and be able to replicate that feel on the course.

If you don't have access to a balance board, try this exercise, using a pole or the longest club in your bag, to help you find your correct posture. Stand up straight with the pole or club touching your lower spine and your head. Now bend forward 25 to 30 degrees, maintaining the touch of the pole or club to the spine and head. Bend your knees slightly. You now have the correct posture for your swing (see figure 3.30).

Figure 3.29 Use a balance board to practice your setup.

Figure 3.30 Determining correct posture.

Here's an at-a-glance view of correct posture:

- As you assume your position, bend forward from the hip sockets 20 to 30 degrees (depending on your balance point).
- Keep your upper and lower spine straight and your head up.
- Bend your knees about 8 to 10 degrees. Your weight should feel light, up on the balls of your feet. I often tell my students to tap their heels up and down to get this feeling.
- Your arms should hang limply from your shoulder sockets (see figure 3.31). Your upper arms should feel as if they're barely touching your chest, but your lower arms should be hanging vertically beneath the shoulder sockets.
- In the correct completed posture, you should be able to draw a line from the top of the spine that intersects the inside of the elbows and bisects the balls of the feet (see figure 3.32). This is your line of balance.

Why spend so much time on posture? Because proper posture allows maximum rotation of the spine and promotes a swing that's 90 degrees to the axis, for the most efficient and fastest swing. Correct posture also determines your balance throughout your swing, the plane or shape of your swing, and your distance from the ball at address.

Figure 3.31 Allow your arms to hang vertically from the sockets to assume the correct posture.

Figure 3.32 Completed posture with the correct line of balance.

Spine Tilt

Just as good posture helps your spine rotate and creates good weight transfer on the backswing, the correct spine tilt to the right also makes the body rotation much easier. In many golfers, there is little or no tilt to the right at address. This position makes it all but impossible to make a good turn and weight transfer.

You can achieve the proper tilt by setting your posture with the back straight and the backside up and then pushing your left hip up and forward toward the target. This will tilt your spine to the right in the correct position. It might feel like you are on an uphill lie, and like your head is behind the ball at address. One word of caution: There is less tilt with shorter clubs than with longer clubs. Without the correct spine tilt, you will come steeply down and across the ball through impact. The spine tilt helps you distribute the weight correctly at address and helps shallow out the downswing.

In a neutral stance, your spine tilt is forward about 25 degrees from vertical; the tilt is from the hip joints. This allows the spine to remain relatively straight up to a point just below the neck. In this position, the body is free to rotate around the spine during the golf swing. The spine must retain a tilted position if the body is going to rotate around it. Poor posture and stance limit the rotation of the spine, and thus the rotation in the golf swing.

To view your proper spine tilt, refer back to the posture exercise illustrated in figure 3.30 on page 53. Note how this position feels so that you can duplicate it on the course.

An element of spine tilt many amateurs neglect is their horizontal tilt, or side tilt of the spine. This tilt is necessary because your head needs to remain behind the ball throughout the swing. See figure 3.33a for a stance with no horizontal spine tilt at address. Most golfers with no preset spine tilt tend to slide their hips on the backswing and lift their arms. This player's head is going to have to move a foot or more to be in position for the beginning of the downswing. Looking at figure 3.33b, notice the golfer's spine is properly tilted to the right at address. Observe this golfer's position carefully. During the backswing his head moves very little to arrive at the proper position for the beginning of the downswing. The golfer in figure 3.33a will have to compensate for a lack of spine tilt by moving the head a great deal over the course of the backswing. The golfer in figure 3.33b won't have to make this compensation because the head, as a result of proper horizontal tilt in the spine, is preset. A mechanically sound golfer can rotate around the spine because the spine is set to the right of center. Review the reverse K position in figure 3.33b. The reverse K position is mechanically correct alignment.

Stance

You can customize your swing significantly by changing the position of your stance within your setup. In general, there are three types of stance—square,

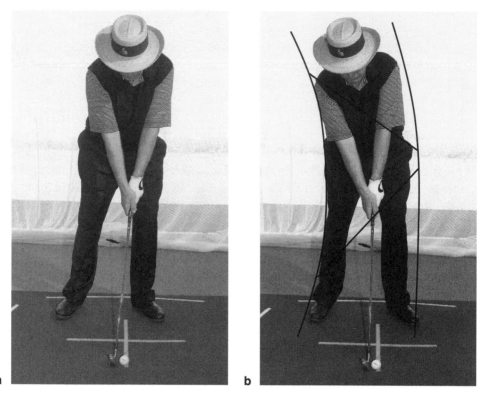

Figure 3.33 *(a)* No horizontal spine tilt. *(b)* Correct reverse K position.

open, and closed—and each one has its own characteristics and link to the swing.

With a square stance, the feet are parallel and left of the target line. The left foot is typically flared slightly, and the right foot is straight (see figure 3.34). The advantage of a square stance is that it allows the body to turn the same amount on the backswing and the forward swing. Also, some players say this stance helps them line up properly, but actually the stance has no bearing on the deflection or curvature of the ball.

With an open stance, a golfer produces a more restricted backswing rotation around the spine but more of an unrestricted forward swing rotation. An open stance is one in which the left foot is drawn back off the target line about two or three inches (eight centimeters) (see figure 3.35). Golfers such as Tom Lehman, Fred Couples, Paul Azinger, Lee Trevino, and Mark Calcavecchia prefer this stance. It restricts the turn on the backswing, creating a tighter coil and making it easier to rotate through onto the left side on the forward swing. In other words, the stance makes for a better coil going back and a faster body rotation and opening up at impact. We use an open stance with almost all short shots to restrict the lower body motion and make it easier to turn through on the forward swing. Also, all short irons should

Figure 3.34 The square stance (also called the neutral stance).

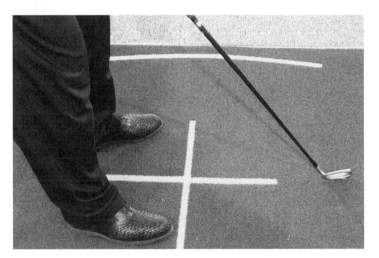

Figure 3.35 The open stance. This stance minimizes lower body rotation on the backswing but maximizes it on the upward swing.

be played with an open stance to tighten up the backswing and make the swing more compact.

The closed stance is a third type of stance, used by Arnold Palmer, Bruce Lietzke, Peter Jacobsen, Craig Parry, and others. This stance produces an unrestricted backswing rotation but a more restricted rotation in the forward swing. The closed stance has the left foot pointed toward the target line two to three inches (see figure 3.36). This stance appears to be aimed slightly to the right. It's most often used by the inflexible golfer who has trouble making a turn on the backswing. This stance allows the golfer to make a good turn on the backswing but seems to stop the turn somewhat on the forward swing. Many golfers who like to hook the ball use this stance,

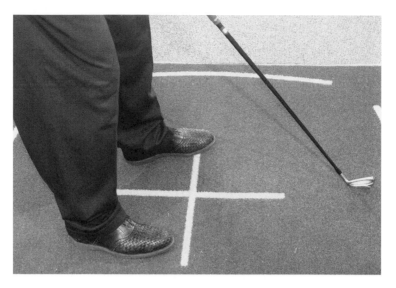

Figure 3.36 The closed stance. This stance maximizes lower body rotation on the backswing but minimizes it on the forward swing.

generally for the driver and longer clubs only. The closed stance allows players to make a bigger turn on the backswing and swing across their bodyline on the downswing. Bigger-chested, inflexible golfers swing this way. Most golfers benefit from using this stance in the right situations.

Four key elements of your stance, no matter which stance you prefer, are stance width, foot flare, weight distribution, and balance.

Stance Width

Your stance width should depend on your degree of flexibility and the club you're using. Flexibility is perhaps the greatest regulator of stance width. For example, if you have very flexible hips and legs, you can have a wide stance. If you're not very flexible in the hips and legs, you'll play best out of a narrow stance. The wider your stance, the more difficult it is to turn your body. The narrower the stance, the easier your body turns. Often, we see players who tend to slide too much in their forward swing go to a narrower stance, which eliminates much of the slide immediately. On the other hand, when a golfer has very loose hip action, as many LPGA and junior players do, I ask him or her to widen the stance and keep the left foot on the ground. This tightens up the leg action on the backswing and develops additional coil in the backswing.

As another example, someone with narrow shoulders and good flexibility might want a wider stance to restrict their natural turn just slightly. Get out on the range and determine what works best for you through trial and error—which is exactly what you and I would do if we were working together. Remember to record your findings and customized positions.

The club you're using should also influence the width of your stance. You want a narrow stance for the short irons and a wider stance for the longer clubs. Any shot that requires stability, a lowered center of gravity, and minimum leg and hip activity requires a wider stance. Uneven lies and bunker shots fall into this category. All golfers can determine the width of their neutral stance by using their natural walking stride and then turning to face the ball (see figure 3.37). Also remember that the outside of the shoulders should be as wide as the inside of the feet in the neutral stance (see figure 3.38).

Another factor influencing your stance width is your swing style. For instance, if your swing is high on the backswing, you'll be leggy on the downswing, which would call for a forward ball position and a wide stance. Or, if your swing tends to be naturally flat, you should probably use a narrower stance to promote more rotary hip action.

I've referred to the width of the feet in relation to the shoulders in your stance. Your stance width depends on your degree of flexibility, the width of your shoulders, and your height. Generally speaking, the width of your stance needs to be the same as your walking stride. Use the following tips to help determine the length of your walking stride:

- Begin walking at a normal pace.
- Once you've established a rhythm in your stride, stop with your stride extended, turn 45 degrees on the balls of both feet, and there you have it: the basic width of your stance for longer clubs.
- Take time to see how this stance width looks and feels to you.

Figure 3.37 Take a natural walking stride and then turn to face the ball to determine your neutral stance width.

Figure 3.38 In the correct neutral stance, the outside of the shoulders and the inside of the feet should align.

In the neutral position, the insides of your feet line up with the outsides of your shoulders. You already know that the distance between your feet helps regulate the amount of turn generated during the swing. The width of your stance also helps to regulate the torque formed by the restriction of the upper body against the lower body in the backswing. The torque you create is another multiplier of the power in your swing. (For more information on torque, see the discussion of turning and coiling in chapter 7.)

Neutral Stance and Muscular Tension

One important aspect of the neutral stance is the amount of muscular tension present during the setup and throughout the swing. Relaxation starts in the setup. You can be certain that your muscular tension at address will be *less* than at any other point in your swing, except perhaps the finish. Scientific law dictates that this principle will hold true in almost every scenario. If you know your muscular tension will tighten from its preswing levels over the course of the swing, it stands to reason that your muscles need to be relaxed at address. Tight muscles cause you to lose the feel of the clubhead, disrupts the flow of energy through your body, and diminishes your ability to produce clubhead speed. Jack Nicklaus always said that when he really wanted to crush a drive, he loosened his muscles even further. Jack knew that loosening up his muscles a little bit at address would give his hands and wrists the additional snap he needed for creating clubhead speed. Take a minute to relax and visualize the image of a crouching tiger. Take in a deep breath, and imagine a poised, relaxed tiger, ready to spring. Stand up, get into your setup, and replicate the feeling in your lower body of being poised to spring.

Create a second image of a powerful gorilla; think of a powerful upper body capable of great feats of strength. Transfer that feeling of power and strength to your upper body. Take the time to close your eyes at address and envision that you have the lower body of a crouching tiger and the upper body of a powerful gorilla. The idea here is to feel your upper body relaxed with hanging arms, much like a gorilla, while your lower body is somewhat tense and ready to spring, like a tiger. How do you feel? Store this feeling for use with your full swing.

Foot Flare

Another important element of your stance is the angle of your feet, called your *foot flare*. In the ideal foot flare position, your feet are either perpendicular to the target line or flared out, as shown in figure 3.39, not pointing in toward the ball.

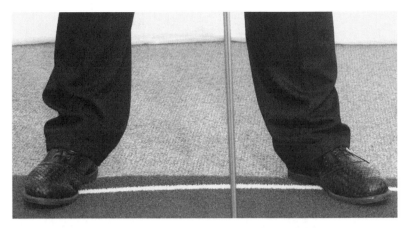

Figure 3.39 Your feet can be perpendicular to the target line or flared out during the stance, as shown.

Both the width of your stance and the amount of foot flare help control the amount of turn in your swing. The degree to which your feet angle out at address fine-tunes the amount of turn you have already preset by the width of your stance. Flexible golfers can keep the right foot in a perpendicular position to the target line because they don't require help in completing their hip rotation. For the more inflexible golfer, flaring the right foot facilitates making a more complete hip turn on the backswing. A player wanting more hip rotation on the downswing can flare the left foot. A player wanting to minimize hip rotation through impact can square the left foot up with the target line. Remember that the knees flex in the direction that the feet are pointed. For examples of how the pros use foot flare see figures 3.40 to 3.43. Here are some more details on foot flare:

• Straight left foot. A straight left foot makes for more left knee and foot movement on the backswing and allows for an earlier posting up on the left leg at impact. This of course causes the club to release a little earlier. A slicer might try a straight left foot to get more hook on the ball.

• Left foot flare. A flared-out left foot restricts the movement of the left knee on the backswing and allows for a little more slide toward the target on the forward swing. Left foot flare also promotes the club releasing later in the impact zone.

• Straight right foot. A straight right foot makes it harder to turn your right hip on the backswing and often causes the right leg to lock out. A straight right foot can also create faster leg action on the downswing by easing the pushoff of the right foot.

• Right foot flare. A flared right foot makes it much easier for an inflexible golfer to turn the hips. This position also allows the right leg to stay somewhat flexed on the backswing. A flared right foot helps a player with fast hips on the downswing to slow the hips, allowing the area to catch up to the body.

Figure 3.40 Loren Roberts has a somewhat narrow stance for such a wide-shouldered golfer so he can make a big hip turn. He plays out of a square stance with both feet flared outward. His left foot flare cuts down on excessive left knee movement on the backswing and allows him to slow his hips down on the forward swing. This gives him time to get his arms down in front of the body at impact. With his right foot flared it's easier for him to turn his hips fully on the backswing while keeping the flex in his right knee.

Figure 3.41 Scott Hoch has an extremely narrow stance with no foot flare. His narrow stance helps him turn his hips. With no flare in his left foot, his left heel is allowed to come off the ground freely. This foot position and his narrow stance all but eliminate excessive hip slide on the downswing while at the same time allowing him to post up his left leg early, causing an earlier release of the clubhead in the hitting zone.

Figure 3.42 Allen Doyle lines up left with his feet to offset his hook. He flares his left foot quite a bit to help him slide his lower body and slow down his hips through impact. This allows Allen to hit his nice, gentle hook.

Figure 3.43 The left foot flare of Corey Pavin helps restrict his hips on the backswing and slows his hips on the downswing.

Keep in mind that the alignment of the golf ball in reference to the left foot is an optical illusion and can thus be misleading. Depending on the amount of foot flare, ball position in relation to your left foot can vary as much as four to five inches (10-13 centimeters). In my teaching, I do my best *not* to refer to the position of the golf ball in relation to the left foot, but you'll notice I fall back into that trap from time to time.

- When the left foot is flared open, the ball appears to be back in the stance (see figure 3.44).
- When the right foot is flared open, the ball appears to be forward in the stance (see figure 3.45).
- When both feet are perpendicular to the target line, the ball appears to be centered (see figure 3.46).
- When you align the ball with your left foot, is it off your big toe or your little toe? This can make four inches (10 centimeters) of difference in your alignment.

It works better to refer to ball position not in relation to the feet but to parts of the chest or upper body. Ball positions range from immediately off the outside edge of the left shoulder to the middle of the sternum. Remember that ball position is relative to the bottom of the swing arc of the club

Figure 3.44 Ball position with left foot flared.

Figure 3.45 Ball position with right foot flared.

Figure 3.46 Ball position with feet perpendicular.

you're using, unless you're hitting from a tee. I'll talk in more detail about ball position starting on page 65.

Weight Distribution

Generally speaking, weight should be distributed evenly between the right and left foot. With the driver there should be slightly more weight to the right side because the stance is wider for this club. In addition, the tilt of the spine to the right is a little more than the other clubs, which puts the head further behind the ball. The feeling with the driver is that the weight is 60 percent right and 40 percent left at address. This puts you in a good position to hit the ball with an ascending (sweeping) blow.

As the club gets shorter, the weight evens out until you get to the 8- and 9-irons and the pitching and sand wedges, where the weight is distributed 40 percent right and 60 percent left at address. This ensures a descending blow. On the shorter clubs, the head is right over the ball and you have less spine tilt at address. The stance is much narrower for the short irons because the swing is shorter.

As far as toe-heel weight distribution, it's important to feel your weight on the balls of your feet at address. The knees are only slightly bent, but the feeling is that the weight is slightly forward. I often tell students to tap their heels up and down at address in order to get the correct feeling. Don't follow the often-heard advice that you should feel like you are sitting on a bar stool at address. This will put the weight back on the heels and you won't be able to move.

Figure 3.47 Static balance drill.

Regarding knee bend, you will see only a slight flex for the average player. The longer your legs are the more flexion you should have in order to lower your center of gravity. The shorter you are, generally the less knee flexion you need. But, you will generally flex your knees more as the club gets shorter. This will ensure stability and less lower body movement.

Balance

A final important part of the stance is static balance. A golfer must be balanced at address or he or she will be trying to balance during the swing. One of the best drills I use for balance is to simply push the golfer backward, forward, and to the right and left during the setup (see figure 3.47). If he moves at all, he is out of balance.

Arm Position

As you are making your setup, it is also important for your arms to be in the correct position. During the setup, the neutral position for the arms is to hang vertically from the shoulder sockets with the hands at a point at which the golf club can be gripped quite naturally (refer back to figure 3.31 on page 54). Correct arm position in the stance is critical. There should be no tension in the shoulders or arms. Tension has ruined more golf swings than I could rebuild in a lifetime. If you were to draw a line from the top of your chin down to the ground, the line should intersect the front of your right hand. In this position, there's plenty of space between the hands and pelvis for your swing, but this space must not be created artificially by extending the hands outward. You want your knees just out of the locked position, with your spine angle such that you can grip the club without making any vertical or horizontal adjustments.

Return to your full-length mirror and check out your stance. Stand up straight, bend your knees, bend forward from both hip joints about 25 degrees, feel like your backside is sticking out, and allow your arms to hang down vertically to a point where the golf club can be gripped automatically. Notice the space between the hands and the pelvis when you're in the correct position.

Ball Position

Just as no one grip fits all golfers, no one ball position suits all golfers. In this section I'll discuss the position of the ball in your stance relative to your swing arc. Because of varying lengths, every club in your bag bottoms out, or reaches the bottom of its swing arc, at a slightly different position in your swing. In theory, you should position the ball so that each club reaches the bottom of its swing arc immediately after it makes contact with the ball. For our purposes here, let's define four distinct ball positions. The driver will be played off the left shoulder, the fairway woods and long irons off the left armpit, the middle irons off the logo on the shirt, and the short irons off the sternum (see figures 3.48-3.51).

Your ball position does change slightly as you work through your clubs from long to short. As clubs get shorter, your stance becomes narrower. As your stance narrows, your swing arc moves back slightly in relation to the center of your body, which is your sternum. As clubs get shorter, shift some additional weight onto the left side of your body. This shift entails that the ball be moved back slightly (on the target line and away from the target) in the stance the shorter the clubs get. Ball position thus varies according to length of the club, width of your stance, and position of your weight.

With longer irons and fairway woods, the width of the stance increases. Remember that the insides of your heels never get wider than the outsides of your shoulders. Also, the outsides of your heels should never be narrower than the width of your hips.

Figure 3.48 Ball position off the left shoulder with a driver.

Figure 3.49 Ball position off the left armpit for fairway woods and long irons.

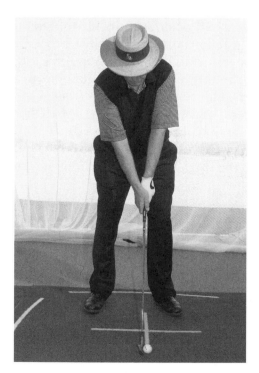

Figure 3.50 Ball position off the logo of the shirt for middle irons.

Figure 3.51 Ball position off the sternum for short irons.

Widening your stance with long irons causes more weight to be distributed over the right side of the body. The position of the weight signals that the ball needs to be moved forward (toward the target) in the stance the longer the clubs get.

Because the ball is struck slightly on the upswing on tee shots, and because the ball is perched on a tee, adjust ball position by slightly moving the ball forward (toward the target) in the stance.

Students often ask about the single ball position of golfers such as Jack Nicklaus, who played all shots off the inside of his left heel. Don't forget to consider that Jack's swing contained a lot of leg drive. His active legs allowed him to play the ball well forward in his stance. Jack also incorporated a slide into his swing for getting over to his left side, which allowed him to use one ball position. He adjusted the amount of hip slide with each club to compensate for using one ball position. Unfortunately, we are not as talented as Jack. Also, golfers who have very little leg drive or very rotary body action will do better with the ball back a little.

Distance From the Ball

Players often ask me, "How far should I stand from the ball?" As you might expect, the answer depends on each unique body type and degree of flexibility. Let your golf club and your body build be measuring sticks for how far you should stand from the ball. For example, if you have a big chest and belly, you should stand farther from the ball with more bend from the hips forward. This gives you room to swing your arms past your body. Or, if you have a thin chest and you are tall, you can stand more erect. Here's an exercise to help you determine how much distance to allow between you and the ball:

- Grip a 5-iron as you would normally.
- Retain your grip as you hold the club out in front of you (see figure 3.52a on page 69).
- Stand tall. Connect your upper arms to your body.
- Bend forward about 20 to 30 degrees.
- Let your arms hang down vertically until your club touches the ground.
- Develop the feeling of supporting the weight of the clubhead with your shoulders.
- Get set in your neutral setup. Bend your knees slightly, as in your regular stance.
- Create the feeling of connecting the upper part of your arms with the upper part of your chest.
- Now, just let your arms hang vertically downward with no tension in either arm.

- Support the weight of the club with the muscles surrounding your shoulders and in your back, not with the muscles in your arms and hands. This is an important feeling in the swing. Can you feel the weight of the club in your shoulders and back? If not, start the exercise over again and work through the process until you can.

- Keeping your arms straight and the club extended, slowly drop your arms as you bend forward from both hip sockets. Allow your arms to drop naturally as you bend forward from the hips.

- Your arms need to hang beneath your shoulders naturally, with no reaching.

- The insides of the upper part of your arms remain in contact with the sides of your chest. Your elbows *don't* touch the side of your chest.

- Keep your weight centered over the balls of your feet.

- As you lower the clubhead down to the ground, have someone place a ball directly in front of the clubface. This is how far to stand from the ball for your physique (see figure 3.52b).

Here's another simple drill to determine how far to stand from the ball. Assume your posture, and hold the club in your left hand only. Now, extend the four fingers of your right hand against your left thigh and left hand (see figure 3.53). This will give a good general distance to stand from the ball.

Finally, you can also determine the correct distance from the ball by bending forward at the hips with the club in your left hand only. Now, just allow the right arm to hang (see figure 3.54). Wherever the right arm hangs is where the right hand should be put on the club.

Body Alignment

Body alignment is the next important element in a good setup, and it can be one of the most confusing elements in the setup for beginners and veterans alike. Many golfers think alignment applies only to the positioning of the feet in relation to the target line. This is hardly the case; in fact, the feet are the least critical element in the entire alignment process.

With normal shots, you *aim* the face of the club straight down the target line. Aim ties in closely with the laws of physics that govern the transfer of energy from the face of the club to the ball. Here's where I usually cover these laws in a golf lesson because I find that once you understand the laws, chances are better that you'll try not to break them.

Body alignment refers to the alignment of the feet, knees, hips, torso, shoulders, and eyes in relation to the target line, with the shoulders and eyes being the most significant. Ideally, all of these lines should be parallel left of the target line, but three of them are more important than the others. For example, your arms, shoulders, and eyes have a direct bearing on how the ball deflects, whereas your hips, knees, and feet have little bearing on the deflection of the ball off the clubface.

a   b

Figure 3.52 *(a-b)* Determining correct distance from the ball.

Figure 3.53 Determining correct distance from the ball by extending the fingers of the right hand between the left thigh and hand.

Figure 3.54 Determining correct distance from the ball using the right arm hang drill.

Key Alignment Terms

This is a good time to make sure we're on the same page with the terms we'll be using when discussing alignment in preparation for further instructions in this chapter and those to come.

Intermediate target line. The top white board (on the right in figure 3.55) represents the intermediate target line. This is the line your ball starts traveling along in relation to the golf hole or to a location on the fairway. I call this line the intermediate target line because you want your shot to start on a straight path down this line and then perhaps curve in another direction toward your intended target.

Path. The line the golf ball travels along to the target is referred to as the ball's path. It is not called a path line, only path. The path can be a straight line all the way to the target but generally curves right or left. You can call this the ball flight path.

Alignment line. The white board by my feet (on the left in figure 3.56) is the alignment line, which is the line I align my body with for the shot. In most full shots, the alignment line is parallel to, but slightly left of, the intermediate target line.

Figure 3.55 The intermediate target line (top board). Aim the bottom of the club at the board

Figure 3.56 The alignment line (left board). Align the body parallel and to the left of the target line

Body or shoulder line. Use a flagstick across the shoulders as an alignment reference line indicating that the shoulders are parallel to the alignment line and parallel but to the left of the intermediate target line (see figure 3.57). This is an important line, and during the course of our lessons I'll be talking from time to time about swinging over the top of the body line. What I'm usually referring to is the golfer swinging out over the top of his or her shoulder or body line, not the target line. This is an important distinction. You can swing out over the body line and still square the blade with the target line. When I'm talking about swinging outside of the target line to back inside, I'll be sure to clarify that distinction for you. Please take special note that the shoulders are usually the most important part of the body to focus on for alignment purposes because the golf swing tends to follow them through the shot.

Alignment. This refers to the relation of the body to the target line. Alignment differs from aiming.

Aiming. This refers to directing the clubface down the intermediate target line. Aim the clubface at your target; align your body perpendicular to your aim. I discuss aim in more detail starting on page 74.

Figure 3.57 The shoulder line. The shoulder line should be parallel and to the left of the target line. The shoulder alignment has the greatest influence on the path of the swing through impact.

A neutral alignment has every one of its alignment points set parallel to, and slightly left of, the target line. Why slightly left of the target line? Visualize a set of railroad tracks. As you look down a set of tracks about 100 yards (91 meters), they remain parallel to each other and never intersect. When you align your body with the track closest to you, your alignment position will be slightly left of the track farthest from you, which is exactly what you're after in your golf swing. The railroad track concept produces the best position for swinging the clubhead through the ball straight down the target line at impact (see figure 3.56 on page 70). Also, because golf is one of the few games played underhanded and to the side of the ball, a majority of players are misaligned without being aware of it. Lining up to the target from a side position *creates* an optical illusion. To better understand what I mean, take a close look at the position of the athletes in figure 3.58, a through d.

Notice that each athlete, except the golfer, is lined up facing the target. If you spend much time playing, or even watching, any of these other sports, there's a fair chance you're lining up incorrectly. Proceed through these steps to check your alignment:

- Get into your setup position over a ball so that you think you're correctly aligned to your target.
- Have a partner set a golf club or bar down across the heels of your shoes to check the alignment of your feet. Your heels should be aligned parallel to and at the left of the target line.
- *Don't* check the position of the toes—foot flare will throw you off; use your heels.
- Have your partner move the golf club up the body line, checking the parallel position of your knees, hips, shoulders, and eyes.
- Now have your partner work back up through these key alignment points, keeping the golf club parallel to and left of the target line, and allow you to move into the correct position in reference to the golf club. Pay close attention to both the feel and look of the correct position. The important thing to remember is that everything is aligned parallel to and left of the target line.
- Repeat these steps in front of a mirror until you've absorbed the feeling of correct alignment.
- Remember, you can't shoot an arrow straight if it is misaligned.

In order of importance in alignment, the shoulders take first prize. This is because the swing path follows the shoulder line. Next in importance are the eyes. Your eyes need to be aligned parallel to and left of your target line as well, but few players emphasize this.

There's one alignment concept I want to reinforce because a lot of players miss it. You'll recall the intermediate target line is represented by the top white board (on the right in figure 3.55 on page 70). This is the line the golf

a

b

c

d

Figure 3.58 *(a-d)* In most other sports, both your body and your eyes line up directly facing the target (straight line game). But in golf the body is lined up to the side, perpendicular to the target (side of the line hitting game). You have to turn your head to see the target, which makes you think you're lined up when you're really aiming off to one side.

ball starts down after impact. You want all shots starting out on a straight target line after impact, or slightly to the right of that line, but *not* to the left. The white board by my feet (white board on the left in figure 3.56 on page 70) represents the alignment line. This is the line I align myself with for the shot. The alignment line is parallel to and left of the intermediate target line. The actual path the ball travels on to the target might be straight, right, or left after leaving the intermediate target line. Alignment and aiming are like shooting an arrow. If you're not lined up correctly, don't expect to hit your target.

Aim

I mentioned earlier that aiming the golf club is not the same as aligning the body. While aiming the clubface seems obvious to most players, you might be surprised at how many players, and good ones at that, misaim the clubface. Physics tells us the clubface must be aligned at 90 degrees to the target line at impact. Unfortunately, it's difficult, if not impossible, to determine if you're aiming the clubface at precisely this angle. However, there are several things you can do to determine if you are, in fact, aiming the clubface properly in your setup routine.

One of the things to pay particular attention to is the bottom one or two grooves of the clubface. Many players make the mistake of aiming their clubs with other parts of the club, including its top line. When the bottom groove or two (see figure 3.59) of the clubface are perpendicular to the target line, the club is aimed properly.

Figure 3.59 Aim the club with the bottom two grooves on the face.

A common aiming problem arises from golf clubs with *forgiving* offsets. Many players have difficulty aiming these clubs because of the offset. If you use offset clubs, it's especially important for you to aim the clubface using the bottom two grooves as your guide.

All good players have a routine they use to line up their clubface and align their body. Here's a tried and true method I use with my students:

- Start from behind the ball. Visualize your general and specific target from here.

- Next, draw an imaginary line from your intermediate target one to three feet in front of your ball all the way to a very specific target 270 yards (247 meters) away. The more clearly you can visualize this line in your mind's eye, the better your chance of making the shot you want to. Now, visualize in detail the flight you want your ball to take.

- Walk up to the ball. Put your club behind the ball with your feet together. At this point, only your right hand is on the club, and your body is very open, looking down the target line.

- Next, take your grip with your feet still together. This is where you're aiming the club with your intermediate target. Take a little step with your left foot and a big step with your right foot to get your stance. Try to keep waggling your clubhead and moving your feet around. Try to keep your body in motion prior to hitting the ball—this gets rid of extra tension. Doing some deep breathing at this time is a good idea.

- Finally, waggle the club a couple of times and pull the trigger.

Watch players like Greg Norman and Tiger Woods, who are very precise in how they set up to the ball. Consider using a magnetic pointer to help you aim the clubface (see figure 3.60, a through c). A pointer is a rod that attaches to the club magnetically, perpendicular to the direction of the clubface. The rod points directly where you're aiming, giving you a much better sense of where you're lining up. Always line up your clubhead first and then align your body at right angles to it.

You've now learned the preswing foundations of a mechanically sound swing. Time for a quick review:

- Grip: Classified as neutral, strong, or weak. Shake hands with your club to get your neutral grip.

- Posture: Proper posture allows maximum rotation of the spine and promotes the most efficient and fastest swing.

- Spine tilt: Tilt spine to the right.

- Stance: Three types of stance: square, open, and closed. The square stance is the neutral stance.

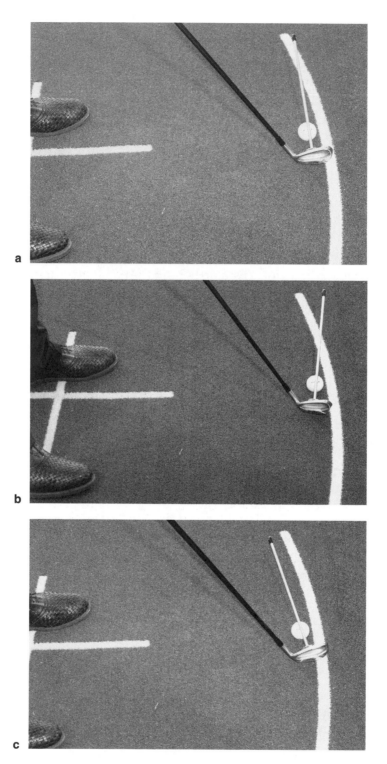

Figure 3.60 *(a)* Square clubface, *(b)* open clubface, and *(c)* closed clubface. Generally, if the clubface or the body are misaimed or misaligned, you will have to make inswing compensations.

- Ball position: There are four ball positions, depending on the shot and club. The driver is played off the left shoulder, the fairway woods and long irons off the left armpit, the middle irons off the logo on the shirt, and the short irons off the sternum.

- Body alignment: Refers to the alignment of the feet, knees, hips, torso, shoulders, and eyes in relation to the target line, with the shoulders and eyes being the most significant.

- Aim: With normal shots, you aim the face of the club straight down the target line.

In the next chapter we'll work through the key positions of the golf swing that follow the setup.

Key Swing Positions

The setup elements of the mechanically sound swing you learned in the last chapter are crucial to finding your perfect swing. The fundamentals and the key swing positions found in this chapter will give you a baseline to start your swing from and a source of objective feedback whenever you need it. Even though you won't swing just like the model, the key positions give you something to revert back to when things go awry.

Most players fall into the trap of making minor compensations during a round or between rounds based on how they feel that day. Instead of getting closer to their ideal swing model they get farther and farther away, which leads to more compensations and a trip to a pro for a lesson to sort things out. If you learn these key swing positions you'll always know where to start from.

Position 1: Neutral Setup

Recall the following positions of a right-hander's neutral setup from chapter 3:

1. Stance—wide as the shoulders
2. Ball position—left heel
3. Head position—behind the ball
4. Foot flare—left foot slightly flared, right foot square
5. Tilted spine—weight 60 percent on right leg
6. Hands—positioned off of inside of left thigh
7. Arms—relaxed and soft
8. Grip—left hand strong with cup in left wrist; right hand facing target
9. Left shoulder—inside of left knee

Now recall the following key elements of your neutral preswing setup (see figure 4.1):

1. Posture—spine straight, chin up, hips bent from 25 to 30 degrees
2. Knees—flexed

a   b   c

Figure 4.1 Position 1: Neutral setup from the *(a)* side, *(b)* down-the-line, and *(c)* rear views. Notice the spine tilt to the right.

3. Weight—on balls of feet
4. Arms—hang vertically from shoulder sockets
5. Alignment—shoulders parallel left
6. Stance—square
7. Eyes—over outside of right hand
8. Line of balance—Draw a line from the top of the spine down to the ground. This line should intersect the inside of the elbows, the front of the knees, and the tips of the toes.

Position 2: Takeaway

Have you ever watched a golfer and knew his or her swing was in trouble a second into the backswing? Your intuition was probably correct because 80 percent of swing problems occur either in the setup or in the takeaway. The takeaway is a critical position in the swing because it's very controllable, and body position changes a tremendous amount within the first foot of the backswing. By the time you get past the first foot or so, most of the good or bad technique has already occurred in the swing.

I focus special attention on the takeaway and backswing for a second reason. They are both slower than the downswing and thus easier to view, analyze, and habituate (make automatic). Because these two aspects of the swing are slower in speed, they are more controllable than the downswing. My philosophy is that when you control the setup, takeaway, and backswing, the downswing and follow-through pretty much take care of themselves. Think of it this way: The setup, takeaway, and backswing are *proactive*, whereas the downswing and follow-through are *reactive*.

In discussing the takeaway, I'll take you through three of the most common techniques I see among good players: the 8 o'clock takeaway, the one-piece takeaway, and the sequential takeaway.

8 O'Clock Takeaway

The technique for the 8 o'clock takeaway goes like this (see figure 4.2):

1. The backswing starts with the upper body.
2. There's no apparent hand or wrist action. The big muscles of the shoulders and torso take the club away.
3. The right arm appears above the left.
4. The left arm maintains contact with the chest.
5. The clubhead is outside the hands, with the club pointing at the target line. Sometimes this is called "hands in, club out."
6. The right arm is slightly extended and above the left.

Figure 4.2 Position 2: The 8 o'clock takeaway from *(a)* side, *(b)* down-the-line, and *(c)* rear views. In *(a)*, note the right arm above the left as the lower body resists the turning upper body. *(b)* Shows the "hands in, club out" position, with the left arm staying connected to the chest. The clubhead points at the target line at all times.

Here's a quick exercise to simulate the 8 o'clock takeaway:

1. After taking your stance, put a club running from your inside left heel to the toe of the right foot.
2. Take the club back. Your club should be directly above the club on the ground (see figure 4.3). This gives the feeling of the club staying in front of the body.

Note that the upper body rotates over stable legs. There's no real shift to the right with the hips. The torso turns, and that turns the hips. Many golfers shift their hips laterally to the right on the early part of the backswing, which is a true swing wrecker because it causes the shoulders to dip and the weight to stay on the left side.

Basically, there are three ways to take the club away: (1) hands first, then arms, then shoulders; (2) arms first, then shoulders; or (3) shoulders and torso first, with big muscles driving the small muscles (called the one-piece takeaway).

Generally speaking, most amateurs use the hands and arms too quickly and too much in the backswing, and the body is not used enough, which results in an over-the-top downswing. For our purposes, it's often best to use the one-piece takeaway, letting the big muscles of the body take the club back.

Figure 4.3 8 o'clock takeaway drill.

One-Piece Takeaway

An alternative to the 8 o'clock takeaway, and the one I prefer in a neutral swing, is the one-piece takeaway. You'll see several players, including Davis Love III and Jim Furyk, using this method. All high swingers prefer this takeaway.

Although there's a great amount of speculation among instructors over which body parts actually move in initializing the golf swing, data generated from the mechanically sound swing model indicated that a one-piece takeaway is the most efficient practice. The model also illustrated that a move back and away from the ball did not trigger the swing. Mechanically sound golfers moved their bodies, if only slightly, toward the target to trigger the swing. This move is commonly called a *forward press*. This slight forward pressing movement is made with the body, not just the hands, and is beneficial for several reasons. First, a forward pressing movement gathers the body in preparation for the action to follow. In most sports, body action is not initiated from a static position. Body action need not be static in golf, either. I can't tell you the number of players who have killed their golf swings by freezing over the ball and allowing tension and negative thoughts to invade their minds and bodies. The gathering sensation is important as well because it mimics the moment of truth, which is the impact position.

This gathering movement gives the brain an impression of where the body and hands need to be when returning to the ball. The forward press position is a closer replica to impact than the original setup position and, because of its dynamic quality, it's easier for the golfer to maintain a feel for the swing than from a static position. When you're able to replicate the feeling of the forward press position through impact, you're on your way to a sound golf swing.

At this point, I'd like for you to put down your book, go get your 5-iron, and work through a drill with me. The steps for executing the one-piece takeaway drill are as follows:

1. Get into your normal setup position.

2. Place the butt of your 5-iron into your belly button as you slide your grip down on the clubshaft.

3. Rotate your chest and stop at an 8 o'clock position in the backswing (see figure 4.4).

4. Keep your right hand on the club and push the shaft out of your belly with your left hand.

There you have it—this is the feel and position of a one-piece takeaway. Now, it's up to you to habituate this feeling and make it automatic.

Figure 4.4 One-piece takeaway drill.

In a one-piece takeaway, it's important to replicate this position with your upper body. The upper body has already started its rotation around the spine by this point, but your lower body is doing very little except remaining in balance over stable legs. Although the hip shift to the right is minor, it's critical in the process of transferring weight over to the right side of your body. Often one simple exercise is worth a thousand words. Here's a procedure to help you create this shift (or a slight "bump," as I refer to it):

1. Put a soccer ball or volleyball between your two arms (see figure 4.5).

2. Take the club back with your shoulders; this replicates the one-piece takeaway. This will get most of your weight to the right leg early in your swings.

Figure 4.5 Use a soccer ball or volleyball to work on upper body turn during the one-piece takeaway. This takeaway is dominated by the shoulders.

Sequential Takeaway

Another way to take the club away is a sequential takeaway. A sequential takeaway refers to the order in which the club, hands, arms, and chest are moved back from the ball—this technique uses sequential motion as a power accumulator in which timing is the primary component. Golfers who prefer a lower, more connected swing prefer to use this method. To accomplish this, they move the clubhead, hands, and arm first; once this movement is complete, the torso and shoulders get into the act (see figure 4.6).

While a typical one-piece takeaway happens together with the shoulders, arms, and club going away together, the typical sequential takeaway's order of movement is (1) clubhead, (2) hands, (3) arms, (4) shoulders, (5) torso, (6) hips, (7) knees, and (8) feet. The order of the movement is then reversed in the downswing. This later body turn generally creates a lower swing and a better coil at the top, so it's more popular on the PGA Tour.

Nick Faldo uses a sequential takeaway. In his takeaway, Nick must be very careful not to overemphasize the role of his hands. The biggest mistake I see in the sequential takeaway is overactive hands. When the hands get

Figure 4.6 Sequential takeaway.

overactive on the takeaway, they're going to be too active on the downswing as well, and now your swing is really in trouble. The hands are involved in the swing for power transfer, *not* for power generation. Overactive hands get a golfer into trouble very quickly because the hands propel the club too far behind the body, and most of the time they come back over the top of the shoulder line. The hands might appear to be initiating the move away from the ball, but they're not controlling it. Regardless of what starts the swing, the big muscles of the shoulders and hips always win the race to the top.

Position 3: Waist-High Back

A checkpoint for transitioning into the backswing is getting the clubshaft parallel to both the target line and the ground. At this position, the arms are at their maximum extension. The left arm is extended, and the right arm is bent. The shoulders have turned about 45 degrees. The lower body (knees and hips) remain stable. The toe of the club is pointing up. The shaft is parallel to the target line. The hands and wrists have done very little up to this point. The right arm is above the left. Most all of this has been done with shoulder rotation, but there has been some forearm rotation to create the toe-up position.

Pay close attention in figure 4.7 to the extension of the hands and arms—they're not folding in but extending. Extension is a power accumulator in your swing because you maintain the radius and arc of the swing. A longer swing radius and arc results in additional clubhead speed through impact. This arc width creates clubhead speed on the downswing.

Figure 4.7 Position 3: Waist-high back from *(a)* side, *(b)* down-the-line, and *(c)* rear views. At this 9 o'clock position, the arms and shoulders have moved but there is very little movement with the lower body. In *(a),* notice that the right arm is above the left, and the slight wrist cock. In *(b),* note that the clubshaft is on plane and parallel with the target line.

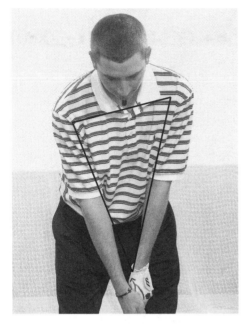

Figure 4.8 Triangle setup.

In figure 4.7 you can see that the left arm remains straight up to this point, but the right arm has started to bend, and the triangle you established during the setup between the shoulders, arms, and hands (see figure 4.8) remains intact. What you can't tell from figure 4.7 is that this position has been created by the big muscles of the upper body. The upper body is more active in the backswing and the lower body less active. Their roles reverse in the downswing.

There's another element that can be seen in figure 4.7—the wrists begin the cocking action about the time they've reached the golfer's right-hand pocket. Before moving on, I suggest you practice swinging several times from this triangle position. You might also want to try the following exercise, using three clubs or flagsticks (see figure 4.9). Put one club or flagstick on the ground, in line with both feet, parallel to the target line. Put another club or stick on your intended target line. Now take the club back and stop at position 3, as we've just described. The club in your hand should be in position 3, parallel to the club on the ground, with your arms in front of the body and the toe of the club pointed up to the sky.

Figure 4.9 Three-club drill for position #3.

Natural Swing Characteristics

The natural swing is perpetual and dynamic. Although there's benefit in practicing key swing positions, be mindful that the swing as a whole is different from each of its parts. Your first move away from the ball must flow, remain on plane, and extend the perpetual motion of the forward press. An effective thought to remember for the swing is, "the arms and hands move up and down, and the body turns around." I mention this because in your initial move away from the ball, the club follows the body rotation to the inside. The pivot of the body takes care of the inward motion of the club, whereas the hands and arms take care of the up-and-down motion of the swing. One of the biggest mistakes I see beginning golfers make is reversing the roles of the arms and body. In the neutral swing, the hands and body move in concert with one another. They begin their respective movements away from the ball at the same time and pace. Grip pressure remains constant with the pressure at address, and because of a light grip, you can sense the weight of the clubhead and the position of the clubface moving back and away from the ball. Your weight begins to transfer slightly toward the inside of your right heel as the clubhead moves away from the ball. If you can't sense the weight on the end of the clubhead during the takeaway, stop and start over again because you're probably gripping the club too tightly and hampering the flow of power through your swing. *The shorter the club, the closer you get to the cup and the lighter your grip pressure becomes.* This is one of my fundamentals.

Position 4: Clubshaft Vertical and On Plane

Your next swing position occurs when the clubshaft is perpendicular to the ground. The butt of the club is pointing down at the target line, the left arm is parallel to the ground, and the clubshaft is vertical. At this point, the hands, club, and arms are still in front of the rotating chest. Once the left arm is parallel, the club should feel vertical. At this point, an on-plane backswing would point the butt of the club at the target line.

At this point in your backswing, you'll feel as if the wrists are fully cocked; the hands, arms, and club are still in front of the body. I call this the L position because the left arm and clubshaft form the letter L. One reason for paying close attention to developing this position is its role in your pitching game. When pitching, the L position is considered the top of your swing.

Notice in figure 4.10 that at this point in the full swing the wrists are set (or cocked). The wrists and folded right elbow form an angle in the swing, thus creating mechanical leverage. Notice the position of the right wrist at this point and the folding action of the right elbow. This action helps maintain

Figure 4.10   Position 4: Clubshaft vertical from *(a)* side, *(b)* down-the-line, and *(c)* rear views.

the correct swing plane for the club. "Folding the elbow" is a vague phrase for some golfers, so I sometimes ask them to think about starting to move the upper portion of their right arm into a parallel position to the ground. Use whatever terminology works for you. At this point in the swing, the shoulders have turned about 60 degrees.

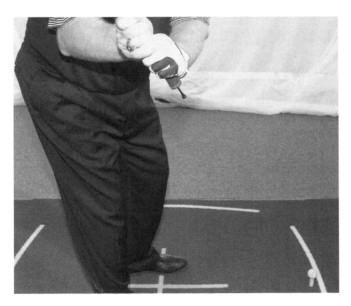

Figure 4.11   Tee-in-the-butt-of-your-club drill.

To ensure you're getting into position 4 correctly, try these two short exercises to develop an on-plane shaft position. First, put a tee in the butt of your club (see figure 4.11). At the L position, make sure the tee points at the ball or slightly inside the ball. Second, put a three-foot extension on the end of an old 5-iron. As you go back, point the shaft extension at the ball (see figure 4.12). This creates an on-plane shaft as well as the correct cocking and hinging of the wrists.

Position 5: Top of the Swing and Transition

The top-of-the-swing position is a critical position in my teaching. There's no one position at the top that's right for everybody, but just like the fundamentals in chapter 3, learning this position now will provide you with a reference point from which to measure your swing. Just remember, all golf swings are different—use these positions as a reference of correctness, not as absolutes. In fact, the very idea of the club being in a position at the top is quite misleading. When we get to the top with the arms, the lower body

Figure 4.12 On-plane shaft drill.

is already going the other way toward the target. So, the club and the body never really come to a stop at the top, but they do slow down before changing direction. This is why the advice to pause at the top is misleading.

The reason that the top of the swing is so critical is there's a "slot" or a "place" in everybody's swing at which the club comes down with a direct route to the ball with a minimum of compensations. This slot, or place, varies widely among golfers. For example, Jim Furyk's position at the top is quite different from Craig Stadler's. For some players, the slot position is quite high, for others it's very flat, and for still others it's very wide. Much of this depends on body build and level of flexibility (which we'll discuss more in the next two chapters).

Here are some of the things to check for at the top of your swing (see figure 4.13):

- Have your shoulders turned 90 degrees and your hips 45 degrees? You should feel as if your left shoulder is turning over the inside of your right leg.
- Have you rotated around your spine and allowed your head to rotate?
- Have your knees and your feet resisted or remained stable on the backswing? Has the right leg stayed in its original flexed position?
- Is the clubshaft close to parallel at the top?

Figure 4.13 Position 5: Top of the swing from *(a)* side, *(b)* down-the-line, and *(c)* rear views. Note in *(a)* the full 90-degree shoulder turn and in *(b)* that the club is on plane with the left arm across the right shoulder and parallel at the top. The spine is angled away from the target because the lower body hasn't moved much in *(c)*.

- Is your upper body weight behind the ball?
- Do the two arms and hands form a triangle at the top?
- Has your left shoulder moved behind the ball?
- Is the shaft positioned outside the right shoulder?
- Is your left wrist flat and in line with the clubface and left arm?
- Is your right elbow pointed down and bent no more than 90 degrees?
- Is your wrist fully cocked at the top?

In nearly every lesson I give, I'll physically put the golfer in his or her correct position at the top. Once we do this, he or she has a direct route to the ball.

As a reminder, at the top of the mechanically sound swing the shaft of the club is parallel to the target line. The clubface is almost vertical, which indicates a neutral clubface position. I often refer to the clubface as being "square" at the top when in this position. Check in your mirror that the back of the left wrist, the clubface, and the left forearm are all lined up. You should be able to determine the position of the clubface at this point in the swing by sensing the position of the back of the left hand without looking at it. Can you do that? If so, that's great. If not, keep working on it.

Check that your upper body is fully turned with a 90-degree shoulder rotation and a 45-degree rotation of the hips, which puts your back facing the target. Your back has moved to this position by rotating around the spine. Observe this position in figure 4.13.

This is a good spot in the swing to check your body position, but what you can't see in figure 4.13 is perhaps the key to this position—the *transition* from the backswing to the downswing. The hips are resisting the rotation of the upper body at this point and accumulating power for the downswing. The golfer's weight has shifted onto the right side of the body, to the right leg, and onto the right heel. The golfer is in the transition phase of the swing because at this point the lower body has already started moving forward. The upper body has coiled around the right hip and is poised for its transition into the downswing. Make a note that coiling is primarily an optional swing technique for accumulating power for the downswing. This is also called separation, but I prefer the term "coiling." Whatever you call it, the lower body is already moving forward while the upper body continues rotating in the backswing and building power.

Watch Champions Tour player Bob Murphy for a good example of this coiling technique. You can see the muscles of his upper body tighten and load up as his lower body starts its turn back toward the target. I'm often asked if there's a pause at the top of the swing. This transition phase is more pronounced in some golfers than in others. Murphy is the "poster golfer" for the pronounced transition—his swing seems to stop at the top, but it really doesn't. His club slows down and appears to stop because his lower body is already moving toward the target while his upper body is still turning back. This is the ultimate stretch or coil, and all great swings have this characteristic.

Make a note in your memory bank that the clubshaft is also accumulating and storing energy during the transition phase. You might frequently hear the term *loading up;* this occurs when you make the shaft flex during your swing, which increases clubhead speed through impact. When executed correctly, the downswing adds additional flex into the shaft. Notice the following in the position at the top of the swing:

- The right wrist is bent back, and the left wrist remains flat; the wrists are set or fully cocked—you should already start feeling the swing transition taking place.
- The shoulders have turned 90 degrees, the right elbow has folded to a 90-degree position, and the right wrist is bent 90 degrees.
- The right elbow is pointing at the ground and at the same angle as your spine.
- The clubshaft is pointing at, or slightly left of, the target.

For just a moment, think ahead to the finish position. Focus on the idea that the position of the hands and arms at the top of the swing is a mirror image of the hand and arms as they travel into the finish of the swing. You can check this out in your mirror or on videotape. Whatever space the hands have at the top of the swing, they should occupy the same amount of space in the finish. Here are additional checks for the top of your swing:

- The upper left arm should remain connected to the chest as the left arm swings across a turned right shoulder.
- The weight should transfer onto the inside of the right heel.
- The right leg should remain flexed.
- Your coil should be over stable legs—otherwise your legs are fighting for balance and become a power drain.
- Extend your left arm to maintain the radius of your swing.
- Cock your wrists and fold the right elbow.
- Load up the shaft by keeping your hands and arms passive by letting the body move the club, allowing the hands and wrists to be reactive to the body movement.
- The width, height, and length of the arc should all affect your power.

One piece of bad advice that has ruined many swings is the thought of pulling the club down like you are ringing a bell. Or, even more detrimental is to jam your right elbow into your side on the downswing, although this is great advice if your favorite shot is a hard hook or a push fade. The right elbow will come into your right hip by impact, but it is a result of the correct lower body action.

The last element critical to the top of the swing is that you develop a position that gives you the most direct and unrestricted path back down to the ball. Finding this position depends on your body build and swing style, which we'll discuss in the next two chapters. The more compensations you must make from the top through impact, the more errors are likely to creep into your swing.

Position 6: The Transition

The transition is a dynamic movement controlled by body movement rather than hand and arm movement. Fortunately, if you move your body correctly, your club will move in the correct plane coming down. Your arms remain passive during the transition, and you should not pull down on the club with your hands (see figure 4.14).

Most of the power is a result of stored energy and using the lower body correctly. At this point, it feels like the feet and the knees are pushing downward into the ground as the weight is starting to transfer to the toe of the left foot. For some golfers this feels like a slight hip bump toward the target. This subtle movement causes the wrists to cock even more as the arms come in close to the body.

Figure 4.14 Position 6: The transition from *(a)* side, *(b)* down-the-line, and *(c)* rear views.

The downswing is initiated and sustained by lower body movement, not by the independent movement of the hands and arms. Sometimes I refer to the transition as separation. It is the point at which the lower body is moving forward while the upper body is staying coiled up as long as possible. Thinking of it this way reminds players to keep their back to the target as their legs move forward and their right shoulder goes downward.

Sometimes the knees move apart during this part of the swing to indicate a correct transition. When the lower body works correctly to change the direction of the club, the club will automatically come down on the correct plane. Think of the upper body being in charge of the backswing, and the lower body as the prime mover on the downswing. If you don't think the lower body is important here, try swinging a club on ice—you'll discover how important the feet, knees, and hips are for correct balance and sequence of motion.

Unfortunately, 90 percent of all golfers start their downswing with an unwinding of their upper body or a casting of the club outward with their hands, wrists, and arms. If more players would remember that there's absolutely no upper body rotation from the top of the swing down through the transition, there would be many more low handicappers out there. Simply feel your right shoulder going down at the ball or tilting slightly backward as your lower body starts transferring the weight to the left side. This side bending is a critical part of all great swings

Figure 4.15 Closed-stance drill.

Figure 4.16 Back-to-the-wall drill.

Try these two exercises for good transition. First, take an extreme or exaggerated closed stance. Put your right heel in the air at address (see figure 4.15). Take the club back straight and bring it down inside the target line. Try to keep the back to the target as long as possible on the downswing as your arms swing down from inside the target line.

Second, stand with your back five inches (13 centimeters) from the wall. Take the club back without hitting the wall (see figure 4.16). At the top of your swing, place the clubhead on the wall. Put pressure on the clubhead and the wall as you run the club slowly down the wall.

Position 7: Into the Downswing

In position 7, the clubshaft reaches a perpendicular position with the ground. If you superimposed the golf swing onto the face of a clock again, the arms would be moving back through the 9 o'clock position. This is a good point to check the swing plane of your downswing: Is the butt of your club pointing at the ball (see figure 4.17)?

The lower body has moved slightly left down the target line and has not

Figure 4.17 Position 7: Vertical downswing from (a) side, (b) down-the-line, and (c) rear views. (a) shows the weight moving to the left as the body hasn't opened up yet. In (b), note the on-plane downswing where the butt of the club points at the ball. Note in (c) the right elbow starting to come closer to the body as a result of the lateral body action.

started opening to the target yet. The weight is on the front of the left foot by this point. The left arm and the clubshaft have either maintained or increased their 90-degree angle from the top of the swing (but definitely not reduced it). Maintaining the 90-degree angle longer than neutral through the downswing creates additional "lag" in the swing. You know you're creating more lag in your downswing when you start thinking to yourself that the club is never going to catch up with the body. You'll feel as if your body, especially your hands, are leading the swing too much. You create a sensation that the club is being left behind. I have to search deep into my own memory bank for the first time I experienced this sensation, but it's still there, and I still work to repeat it. If you don't learn to create the sensation of lag, you'll never be as consistent a ball striker as you'd probably like to be—nor will you realize your potential for creating distance.

By this position in the downswing, your right elbow appears to be coming in closer to the body; the left arm is straight, thus maintaining the radius of the swing. Here's an exercise to practice this feeling. Tie a towel to the end of your driver and swing your club this way 25 times a day for two weeks (see figure 4.18). This will create more lag, or leverage, in your downswing and thus more distance.

When you reach position 7 you'll feel as if your belt buckle is facing the ball because your hips have not yet rotated. I call this "centering your pivot." The right shoulder is continuing to go down toward the ball as the right elbow is starting to slip in front of your right hip. At this point, the arms should feel soft and close to the body. The shaft should be positioned between the right shoulder and right elbow to be on a perfect plane, with the butt of the club pointing at the ball.

Figure 4.18 Towel drill to create more lag in your downswing.

Position 8: Parallel to the Ground

I call position 8 the "delivery point" because it occurs when the clubshaft has returned to a parallel position to the ground. The shaft is also parallel to the target line, moving down the target line but remaining a little inside so that it doesn't cross it. The hips now look as if they're finally opening up toward the target. The shoulders are still square, and the hips are leading into the downswing. Notice in figure 4.19 how the hips, hands, arms, and shoulders are in front of the clubhead. The upper body leads the parade up; the lower body leads it back down.

The upper body does not catch up with the lower body until just after impact. Following impact, the upper body outrotates the turn of the lower body and passes it. Observe in figure 4.19 how the wrists are still cocked. All mechanically sound golf swings have the left wrist ahead of the clubface in this position and through the impact area. The clubface is approaching the ball from inside the target line.

During the downswing, the right shoulder moves down toward the ball to help keep the arms and hands in front of the body. You'll recall that keeping the arms in front of the body is a fundamental. Think of the spine actually tilting slightly downward, away from the target and under as the hips shift forward and open up during the downswing. Try this exercise for getting into position 8. Put a padded golf shaft about one yard (one meter) behind your ball. Practice coming inside of that shaft without hitting it (see figure 4.20 on page 101).

Position 9: Entering the Impact Zone— Preimpact

Just prior to impact, you can pick up from watching videotape of your swing that your hips are opening toward the target, your right heel is starting to come off the ground, and your left hand is in front of the ball (see figure 4.21 on page 101). By advancing the frames of the video, you can see your lower body continuing its turn and your upper body rotating back around the spine. The club is coming from the inside of the target line and on the swing plane of the backswing. Your upper body is rotating very quickly but has not yet caught up with the lower body. Your head remains in position behind the ball. To help you visualize position 9, think of swinging under an imaginary bridge.

Figure 4.19 Position 8: Delivery point from *(a)* side, *(b)* down-the-line, and *(c)* rear views. Note in *(a)* how the hips are starting to unwind as the body and hands stay ahead of lagging clubhead and how the wrists stay cocked far into the downswing. In *(b)*, the club is approaching from inside the target line.

Figure 4.20 Use a padded golf shaft to practice position 8.

a   b   c

Figure 4.21 Position 9: Preimpact from *(a)* side, *(b)* down-the-line, and *(c)* rear views. Note in *(a)* that the hands are ahead of the clubhead as the arms come in front of the body, and the head is behind the ball. In *(c)*, note how the head and spine are tilted right, and how the right heel is off the ground.

Position 10: At Impact

At impact, most of your weight has shifted over to your left side and is turning around the left heel. Your club must be coming down on a shallow angle of approach. The hips have opened to about 40 degrees while the shoulders are open only about 20 degrees. At impact the best club swingers try to close the gap between the shoulders and hips at impact. In other words, they try to get the chest and upper body caught up to the lower body by impact. Your head remains behind the ball. Your left leg has straightened (or "posted up"), and your right heel is slightly up in the air. Your right arm is extended, with the right forearm behind the shaft. Notice in figure 4.22 that the right wrist is bent, the left wrist is straight, and the hands are slightly ahead of the clubhead. Mechanically, all great players have a flat left wrist and a bent right wrist at impact, due in part to the fact that the shaft of the club is still positioned slightly forward in the swing. For most golfers, this position is pretty much opposite of the setup position. In the setup, the left wrist is cupped and the right wrist is flat. I can tell you that all great ball strikers have a flat left wrist at impact. In all of my lessons, I work to match up the grip as it goes through the forward press with the golfer's impact grip.

The impact position of the swing is important enough that in many lessons I teach this position to a student right up front. The 6 inches (15 centi-

Figure 4.22 Position 10: Impact from *(a)* side, *(b)* down-the-line, and *(c)* rear views. Note in *(a)* the hands are ahead of or even with the clubhead at impact, in *(b)* the chest catching up to the hips, and in *(c)* the head and spine behind the ball at impact.

meters) immediately before and after impact are perhaps the most important 12 inches (30 centimeters) in the golf swing. You'll recall from chapter 1 that the goal of the golf swing is to deliver the clubhead to the ball perfectly square to the target line, perfectly vertical, so that only the loft of the club affects the trajectory of the shot, with maximum velocity at the bottom of the swing arc, and on a consistent basis. Notice in figure 4.22 that the shoulders are open slightly and that the hips have turned more than the shoulders have rotated. The right elbow has straightened and appears to be either on or in front of the right hip. Try this exercise to practice the impact position. Buy an impact bag or get an old bag and stuff it with towels. Swing at the bag 25 times a day, focusing on keeping your hands ahead of the clubhead (see figure 4.23). You can also press a club against a desk to simulate the impact position. Another exercise is to hit 40-yard (37-meter) punch shots and hold your impact each time (no follow-through).

Figure 4.23 Use an impact bag to practice the correct impact position with the hands ahead of the clubhead.

Position 11: Postimpact

Position 11 occurs just after impact, at which point the rotation of the shoulders carries on through the swing, catching up with the hips, while the lower body is slowing down. The right arm is completely extended (see figure 4.24). This is the point at which the clubhead reaches its maximum velocity. The left wrist is still flat, and the right wrist is beginning to bend. I can always recognize great ball strikers when they are in this mechanically sound position. To find the postimpact position, put a ball four inches (10 centimeters) in front of your left heel and slightly inside the target line. This will show how the club arcs back to the inside after impact (see figure 2.4 on page 16 for an inside-to-inside path).

Position 12: Extension

This position is also called the release point. What's really apparent in this position is how the right hand is completely released and on top of the left hand. You can also see in figure 4.25 that the right arm is completely extended, the club looks like an extension of the hands and arms, the right shoulder has gone down and under the head, the left arm is folding in toward the body, and the torso is catching up with the hips. The club is still on plane. The side view of this position shows that the club is following the

Figure 4.24 Position 11: Postimpact from *(a)* side, *(b)* down-the-line, and *(c)* rear views. The club and left arm are in a straight line as the hands and club follow the rotation of the body.

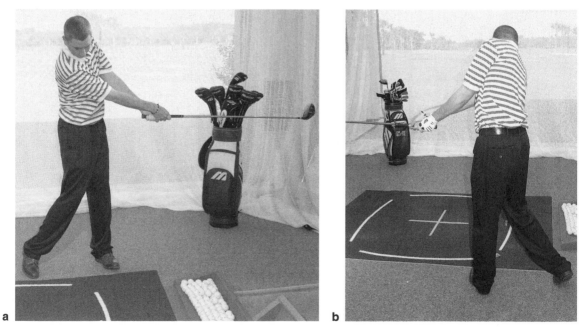

Figure 4.25 Position 12: Extension from *(a)* side and *(b)* rear views. Note that both arms are straight as the right hand is on top of the left, showing a complete release.

rotation of the body. The club is still in an arching motion, which has been inside of the target line on the backswing, down the line at impact, and inside the target line on the follow-through.

Here are several exercises to help you find and get into the extension and release position:

- Split grip—Put your right hand three or four inches below your left. Take swings to practice your release and extension (see figure 7.20 on page 189).

- Back to the target—Address a ball with your back to the target. Hit balls this way to feel your release.

- Slicer's special—Close the face at address. Force the toe of the club to get to the ball first to feel the correct release.

- Toe to toe—Toe up at the waist-high back position and again at the release point.

- Plane board—Put your club on a plane board and leave it there after impact (see figure 4.26). This shows how the club follows the turn.

Figure 4.26 Use a plane board to practice an on-plane extension position.

Position 13: Clubshaft Vertical Again

The clubshaft is vertical for the third time when the club is in this position. The left arm continues to fold up as the wrists recock on the forward side of the swing. This recocking helps weaker golfers achieve some clubhead speed. I like to show students this position because it should be a mirror image of the same point in the backswing. When players are out of position on the backswing, they're usually out of position here as well. Although this position in the swing is unfolding too quickly to be controlled, you can certainly control its mirror image position during the backswing. Faults in the backswing and setup are reflected in this position.

Notice in figure 4.27 that the right foot is almost up onto the toe of the shoe, the belt buckle is either pointing down the target line or is almost there, the left elbow is bending, the wrists are cocking again, and the upper body is passing the lower body. To help locate and feel this position, stand next to a wall. Measure off your normal extension point with your right arm extended at position 12. Now swing without hitting the wall. This helps your wrists recock on the forward swing.

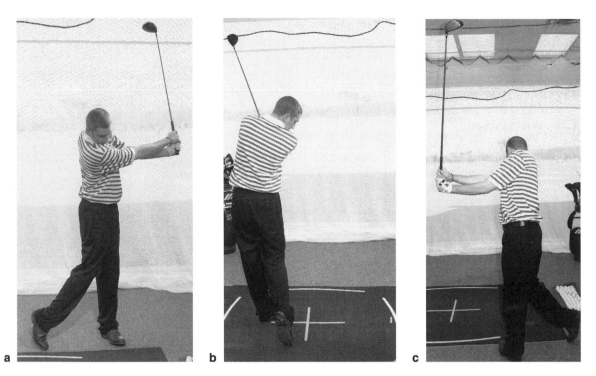

Figure 4.27 Position 13: Vertical follow-through from *(a)* side, *(b)* down-the-line, and *(c)* rear views. In *(a)*, you can see the head starting to come up as the wrists are recocking upward. In *(c)*, note how the left elbow folds down to the ground at this point.

Position 14: The Finish

Your head should be looking directly at the target in your finish and in a position over, or immediately behind, the left heel, but not ahead of it. Note in figure 4.28 how straight the left leg is. Also look at the position of the hips in relation to the legs. The left elbow is pointed down to the ground and is behind the golfer

When you're relaxed through your swing and allow the momentum of the club to carry through, the club will end up resting on your back with soft and relaxed hands. If your club finishes pointing toward the sky, tension in your arms has probably restricted your finish. If your finish doesn't look like the one shown in figure 4.28, it's pretty certain that you've leaked power somewhere in your swing.

In the finish position, the chest is facing left of the target line; the hips are parallel to and left of the target line. The knees have come together and are touching. The right heel is up in the air in a vertical position.

I always remind students to finish at their full height. Whatever your height is when you're standing straight up, this should be the height of your finish. Don't finish with your weight still back on your right side. You should finish with your head over your left leg and your body in an I position (see

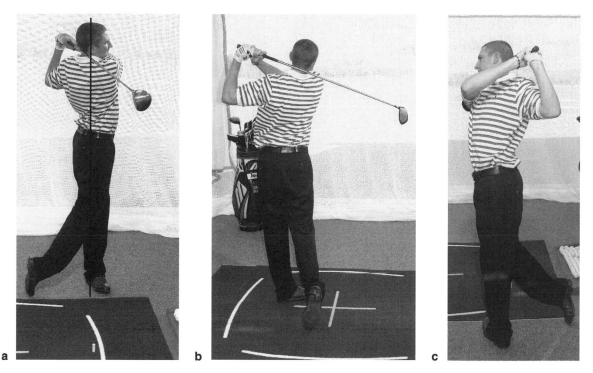

a   b   c

Figure 4.28 Position 14: Finish from *(a)* side, *(b)* down-the-line, and *(c)* rear views. In *(a)*, see how the head is positioned over the left leg with the knees together. In *(b)*, note how the arms are relaxed with the club behind the neck, and in *(c)* how the eyes face the target at the finish.

figure 4.29a), or close to it. Avoid finishing in a reverse C position (see figure 4.29b), which is a result of driving your legs hard and swinging excessively inside to inside. Yes, it looks nice, and it's the finish you often see on TV these days, but it's also the position that drove Johnny Miller, Jack Nicklaus, and thousands of other golfers to the back doctor before their time.

Key Position Exercises

Try any or all of the short exercises that follow to help you find, feel, practice, and refine the key positions we've covered in this chapter. When appropriate, use a full-length mirror to check your progress on each of the positions you work on. At this stage in your development, a mirror image is better than videotape. Video feedback is more valuable when you're making your swing at full speed.

- In sequential order, work through and hold each of the key swing positions for three to five seconds each. Feel relaxed in the position; focus on the feeling of each position. Remember, all swings are a little different, so you shouldn't be frustrated if you can't get into all of these positions exactly as described. The positions serve as a reference of correctness

Figure 4.29 *(a)* I position; *(b)* reverse C position.

and not as an absolute. As we go further into the book, we'll discover what your body will let you do.

- If you have the strength, use a weighted club to help expand the feel of the positions and enhance your training experience. Always take care not to overexert yourself when swinging a weighted club. Stop immediately if you feel any pain or undue stress.

- Once you've done the previous exercise, take your weighted club and make full swings in slow motion, paying special attention to each of the key positions as you move through them.

- Switch to your 5-iron and take slow-motion swings until you feel each key position and can repeat it on demand.

- Take regular full swings with your 5-iron. Have a friend videotape your swing so you can compare your swing to the key position photos shown in this chapter.

- Focus on the kinesthetic position of your body as you work through each position. You can do this by closing your eyes and feeling each position for a count of 5 or 10. (Do remember that it's only important for you to know these positions for conceptual purposes. In actuality, you swing *through* the positions. You might want to copy the position at the top, but I want you thinking about one fluid move through your swing.)

At this point in your reading, you know how to analyze your current swing; you have learned the setup foundation for a neutral swing; and you have a good sense of the 14 key positions of the golf swing. It's now time to locate your dominant physical power source, which we'll do in chapter 5. This will give you a guideline to help you develop your own swing.

5

Swing Power Sources

You've seen the pros coming down the 18th fairway with a chance to win a tournament. These players are using their natural power source. And, what's more interesting is that players rely on different power sources. If you try to rework your swing against your power source, you'll always be fighting your natural swing, and your forced swing will break down under pressure. The key is learning to build your swing around one (or a combination) of the natural power sources, which include the upper body, the lower body, the hands, and the gifts of exceptional rhythm, timing, and balance.

Power sources come in two types: physical and mechanical. Generally, the mechanical power sources are those mechanics that you've learned when you learned your swing. They are highly dependent on your physical power sources and what your body will let you do. I will talk about mechanical power sources later in chapter 6.

To craft your perfect swing, you'll need to determine your own dominant power source and build your swing around it. Read through the attributes for each power source discussed in this chapter, and then try the tests. Remember that the criteria are not absolutes. You might have some characteristics that belong in more than one power source, but in my long years of teaching I've found that everyone fits best into one of the four categories. What you're trying to find is the *best* fit for your swing, which you can use as a base from which to work. Your base gives you the solid fundamentals to return to when things go wrong. In the next chapter, you'll match up with a pro model to reinforce these fundamentals. Once the fundamentals are in place, you can make adjustments based on such variables as ball flight preferences or how you're swinging on a given day. Your fundamental base itself doesn't change—you only adjust it as your body changes.

Dominant Physical Power Sources

Your physical traits determine your best power source. To find your dominant power source quickly, read through the general attributes listed in this section and, if you find a good fit, go straight to the section dealing with that particular power source. If you fit more than one of these traits, or if you're not sure which one applies, read through all the power sources to find the one that fits best.

The four dominant power sources are the upper body, the lower body, the hands, and an unusually high degree of rhythm, timing, and balance. For convenience, I call this last category "Classic Swinger" or balanced player because he or she uses a fine swing and timing to produce power.

• Upper body players generally have shorter than normal arms, so they access their power through their strong shoulder and back muscles. Craig Parry and Craig Stadler fit into this category. If you fit this category, see the following section to read more about upper body players.

• Lower body players tend to be over 71 inches (180 centimeters) in height for men or over 66 inches (168 centimeters) for women; they are athletic and tend to have long legs, which they use to generate power throughout their swing. If this sounds like you, go to page 114 to read more about lower body players.

• Hands players usually have large hands and forearms that provide the strength and coordination to increase swing speed through impact. Many players over the age of 50 fit into this category, as they use their hands to make up for lost strength and flexibility. Sound like you? Go to page 119 to read more about hands players.

• If you've been called a "natural" because of your smooth, effortless, and balanced swing and if you have long arms and are extremely athletic, you likely fit into the final category, Classic Swingers. If this sounds like you, turn to page 121 to read more on using your gifts of rhythm, timing, and balance as your primary sources of power.

In the following sections, we'll look at each of the four types of dominant physical power sources in more detail and have you try some tests to assess some of your physical attributes; this will help you determine which of the power source categories you best fit into.

Upper Body Players

The typical dominant physical characteristics of upper body players are a thicker than average chest and wider shoulders, muscular upper body and arms, a long torso, shorter than average arms and legs, and below average upper body flexibility. These players generally range from 64 to 68 inches (162-172 centimeters) in height. Some upper body players are Arnold Palmer, Duffy Waldorf, Meg Mallon, Craig Stadler, Hal Sutton, Laura Davies, Bruce Lietzke, Joey Sindelar, and Craig Parry.

Upper Body Flexibility Test

Upper body flexibility determines the length of your swing and how you set up to address the ball. To assess your flexibility, try the following test:

Sit on the edge of a stool or exercise ball with a bar resting across your shoulders parallel to the ground. As you turn to your right as far as you can without turning your hips (see figure 5.1), have someone record how many inches or centimeters the club turns. Perform the same movement to the left and again have someone record the amount of torso rotation.

Notice that the straighter your back and spine, the farther you can rotate your torso (remember this during your golf swing: flexibility creates speed). How did you measure? If you moved the club less than 90 degrees, you have below average upper body flexibility, which might place your dominant power source in the upper body category. If you moved the club more than 90 degrees, your upper body flexibility is average or above, which means your dominant power source is likely *not* your upper body. Upper body players can't rotate a full 90 degrees on the backswing, so they have to use their upper body and arms early on the downswing. They are more right-sided players, or what I call "hitters."

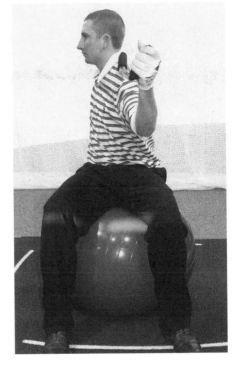

Figure 5.1 Upper body flexibility test.

Most people have more flexibility in one direction than another. If you're a right-handed golfer and you're more flexible turning to the right, consider using a slightly more open stance to help you turn better to the left. If you're more flexible to the left, a slightly more closed stance will keep you from overrotating through the swing and allow your right side to turn more easily on the backswing.

Figure 5.2 Arm swing test.

Arm Swing Test

Your arm swing will be determined by how big your chest is and how bent over from the hips forward you are at address. To assess the amount of forward bend from your hips, try the arm swing test. Raise your left arm up in front of your body to chest height (not shoulder height, but to chest height at about your pecs). Without bending your elbow or wrist, move your left arm toward the center area of your chest (your sternum) until you feel the inside of your arm being restricted by your chest (see figure 5.2). Once you feel restricted, don't force your arm over toward the center any farther.

Keeping your left arm in place in front of your body, now raise your right arm up and again to chest height at about your pecs. Without bending your elbow or wrist, move your right arm toward the center area of your chest until you feel the inside of the arm being restricted by the chest. Again, don't force your arm farther toward the center once you feel restricted.

If your right hand does not make it over to your left hand, you have a larger than average chest and are most likely an upper body player and will have to bend forward a lot in order to get enough arm swing.

If you fit this category, your physique is generally designed for a flatter and relatively short backswing with less leg action. Some upper body players are so tight in the shoulders and chest that they can't rotate through a short swing. To generate extra shoulder turn, lift your arms and let your right elbow "fly" more than normal. Hal Sutton, Craig Stadler, and Joey Sindelar use this type of swing motion to generate more power.

Lower Body Players

The typical dominant physical characteristics of lower body players are strong legs (some are long, some are stocky, but they must be strong), shorter torsos, moderate to good flexibility, long arms, taller than average height (the greater your height over 69 inches [175 centimeters], the more likely you are to be a lower body player), and above average athleticism. Some lower body players are Tiger Woods, Paul Azinger, Scott Hoch, Juli Inkster, Fred

Couples, Davis Love III, Karrie Webb, and Jack Nicklaus (particularly in his early days). You find many lower body players on the LPGA Tour because women's legs are often the strongest parts of their bodies.

As you might expect, the signature of the lower body player is leg action. Lower body players can always be identified by how hard the lower body appears to be working. Leg action is related to the action and movement of hip rotation. Generally, the speed of hip rotation allows a golfer's legs to transfer energy to the hands and arms. Whereas the upper body player has a relatively smooth and even leg motion as the swing unwinds, the swing of the lower body player stresses knee and ankle movement, sometimes making the swing look more awkward or "jerky" than the more fluid swing of the Classic Swinger.

How the Lower Body Works for the Lower Body Player

As the shoulders and arms take the club back in a one-piece takeaway, the weight moves into the inside of the right heel. Then, at the top position, the shoulders turn 90 degrees to 110 degrees and the hips turn about half that much.

During the downswing and transition, the weight moves very aggressively into the left toe. This gives the appearance that there is a gap between the knees and the hips and that they have moved laterally toward the target. The right elbow then reconnects with the right hip. At this point, the weight is not only moving into the left leg, but the weight is also going down into the ground so the player can push off the ground for his power.

Just before impact, when the club is in position 8, the hips start to spin. This delays the club and keeps the wrists cocked until the last possible moment. The golfer pushes off the ground very hard at this point. The left leg posts up as the centrifugal force of this rotational speed of the hips create the golfer's power.

It is probably more difficult to alter your natural leg action than it is to change anything else in your swing. Of the players I know, Nick Faldo came the closest to making significant changes in the action of his legs. He always had a high swing with a lot of leg action coming down. In working with a skilled instructor, Nick lowered his swing and quieted his legs down a little, though he still retained a very leggy look through impact. The tradeoff that occurs in most mechanical changes in the golf swing involves distance versus direction. Nick wanted to gain accuracy, so he went to a lower swing with less leg drive. As a result, he lost some of his natural distance. He succeeded in changing his leg action in part, and his shots did become more accurate, but he still has some of his natural slide, which is one reason I say leg action is so difficult to change.

To assess your lower body flexibility, try the leg over, spinal rotation, and hamstring flexibility tests.

Leg Over Test

Lie flat on your back with your legs extended and both arms extended straight out to the sides. Let your right leg swing over your body until it touches your upper left leg (see figure 5.3). As you're doing this, rotate your head to the right. Try to keep your right arm on the ground while you perform this movement. Hold the position for 30 seconds; then repeat with your left leg, rotating your head to the left.

If you can't comfortably move one of your legs over your body to touch the other leg, you're not flexible enough to be a lower body player.

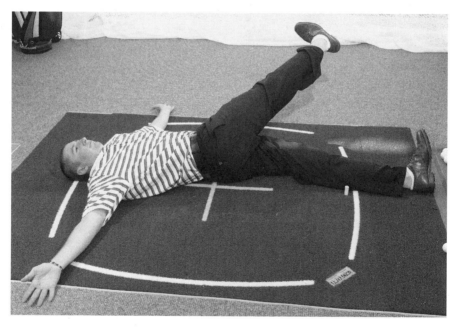

Figure 5.3   Leg over test.

Spinal Rotation Test

Lie on your back with your arms extended straight out to the sides and your legs bent at the knees in the air. Slowly lower your legs to one side (see figure 5.4) until your knees are together and on the floor. If you have normal spinal rotation, your knees will touch the floor without the opposite shoulder coming off the ground. If you can't comfortably touch your knees to the floor without lifting your shoulder, you have poor rotation, which means that during your swing you can't coil against your hips. Rather, your hips move with the rotation on the backswing and forward swing, resulting

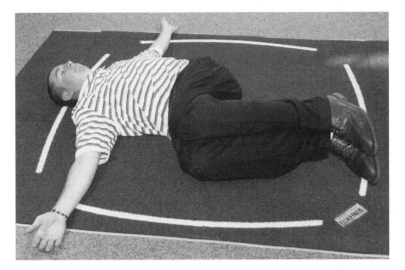

Figure 5.4   Spinal rotation test.

in a loss of power. You need good spinal rotation to use your lower body effectively, so if you can't touch your knees to the floor without lifting your shoulder during this test, you're probably not a lower body player.

Hamstring Flexibility Test

Sit on the floor with your legs fully extended about 30 inches (76 centimeters) apart and lay a club across your shins (see figure 5.5). Reach forward, keeping your legs straight. Mark on the floor the point at which your fingers reach. If you can reach past the club, you have good flexibility in your hamstrings and are more likely to be a lower body player.

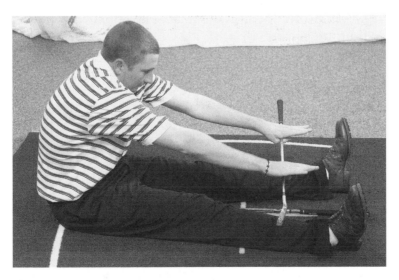

Figure 5.5   Hamstring flexibility test.

Figure 5.6 Tiger Woods demonstrates his natural aggressive leg action that he learned as a junior.

Tight hamstrings mean poor posture because the pelvis is not able to rotate forward. This creates excessive bend in your lower back, limiting spine rotation and the proper use of the legs. To compensate for tight hamstrings, the body is forced to use the arms more.

Tiger Woods' swing illustrates that fast legs work within the lower body category as well as powerful legs (see figure 5.6). Tiger uses his legs extensively through his swing. He coils his upper body against the resistance of his legs on the backswing and drives his legs hard on the forward swing. He was taught to swing this way as a junior, partly because his legs were the strongest part of his body. Since coming out on tour, he has been trying to quiet his legs down on his downswing.

You can't always tell by looking just how strong a person's legs are. Leg muscles can be very powerful for both men and women. Players with long legs, such as Tom Lehman, also tend to use their legs in squaring the blade at impact. Such players tend to have a pronounced slide to their hips and legs on the downswing. Look at tall players, such as Jim Furyk, and how leggy they are on their downswings. Even at the professional level, I think these players need to work on swinging over more stable legs with a more centered pivot on the backswing. They need more turn, and less hip slide, in the downswing.

Golfers with long legs must be very careful to keep their legs quiet and stable on the backswing. Long-legged golfers always seem to have problems sliding too much both back and through, whereas short-legged golfers seem to have an easier time just rotating their lower body. Also, the long-legged golfers have to flex their knees more at address to get their center of gravity lower and keep their balance. Compare Ian Woosnam's rotary hip and leg action to Jim Furyk's sliding leg action—these are two distinctly different ways to move the lower body.

Another factor that can significantly affect the swing is height. Tall golfers usually swing higher. If you're tall, you have to bend forward quite a bit to get your club on the ground, and you'll have to bend your knees more than the average golfer.

If you're a lower body player, you don't swing your club around your body as much as upper body players do. At the completion of your backswing, the clubshaft will be more or less directly above your right shoulder. Overall, the club should be swung on a wide and high arc, which is much different from the flatter and wider backswing of an upper body player.

You can also check your ball flight to see how well you fit into this category. Many lower body players tend to hook or draw the ball because of their hand action at the bottom of the swing. Jack Nicklaus used leg drive but compensated in other parts of his swing to turn his ball flight from a draw to a high and left-to-right fade. Jack lined up with an open stance, swung the club high above his head, and quickly rotated his hips through impact to produce his trademark

Figure 5.7 Notice how open Juli Inkster's hips are at impact. This is a trademark of the lower body player.

fade. For the typical player, however, it's very difficult to master so many compensations that work against natural ball flight.

Most players on the LPGA Tour use their legs more than their male counterparts on the PGA Tour because their legs are the strongest parts of their bodies. Juli Inkster is a good example (see figure 5.7). She has very long, strong legs and has always based her timing on leg action on the downswing. The average female club player would do well to imitate the way LPGA players use their legs.

Hands Players

The typical dominant physical characteristics of hands players are extremely good eye–hand coordination, strong hands and forearms, large hands with long fingers, below average flexibility, and quick, sensitive hands. Corey Pavin, Marisa Baena, Seve Ballesteros, Chi Chi Rodriguez, Hubert Green, John Bland, and Dave Stockton are examples of hands players.

Hands players can be found among the ranks of golfers with thin physiques and hands that don't look obviously powerful in and of themselves. For hands players, the key to success is quick movement, especially through the impact zone. Hand speed through impact generates additional clubhead speed and makes up for a lack of physical bulk in the upper body, arms, and legs.

Many players on the Champions Tour (what used to be the Seniors Tour) are hands players because as their bodies get older and they lose flexibility, they work their hands into the mix as a power source. Although Marisa Baena, a small woman with quick hands, probably fits into this category, on the whole you don't see a lot of hands players in the LPGA because most women don't have the hand strength required to generate power.

If you think you might fall within the category of hands players, assess your hand and wrist strength by doing the hand strength test and wrist strength test.

Hand Strength Test

If your hands are to be your dominant power source, they need to be larger and stronger than average. For this test, use a small rubber ball or a tennis ball. If you can squeeze the ball tightly more than 60 times without fatiguing your forearms, chances are good that you can use your hands as a power source.

Wrist Strength Test

With your arm extended and a golf club in your hand, rotate your forearm and wrist to the left and then back to the right (see figure 5.8). If you can do 10 repetitions, your forearms and wrists are quite strong. To confirm the results, try holding a 10-pound dumbbell and extending your forearm over a bench. Simply bend and extend your wrists until fatigue sets in. If you can do 50 reps before tiring, your wrists are quite strong. You might fall best into the category of hands players.

Figure 5.8   Wrist strength test.

All hands players have to be concerned about hooking their shots out of play. Thus, the great majority of today's top golfers try to eliminate overreliance on the hands. Your hands are more difficult to control than other power sources in terms of consistency and accuracy through the high speeds of impact, especially under pressure. Some of the older players on tour grew up relying more on their hands because of the inconsistencies in golf equipment and shafts. They had to adjust to each shaft individually. As shafts and equipment improved, modern players have gotten away from using their hands in an attempt to square the blade through impact and to compensate for inconsistencies in equipment.

Modern-day golfers can also afford to move away from their hands as a power source because they have become larger and stronger physically. It has helped that equipment and golf courses have improved as well. The demand for distance on more and more courses has moved players toward getting their bodies into their swings. Today's average golfer, even if not as well conditioned or as large as the tour professional, has the advantage of improved equipment—better shafts and balls—to help generate optimal power without relying too much on the hands.

Classic Swinger and Modern Swinger

The dominant physical characteristics of the Classic Swinger are balance throughout the swing; well-coordinated, easy-to-synchronize body movement; gifted physical skills allowing for a variety of shots; smooth rhythm with a relaxed tempo; long arms and a thin chest; good flexibility; and good spine rotation. Vijay Singh, Mark O'Meara, Sam Snead, Phil Mickelson, Larry Mize, Al Geiberger, Loren Roberts, and many of the players on the LPGA Tour are Classic Swingers.

Classic Swingers have the gift of superb overall coordination and tend to be tempo driven in their swing. They generally don't rush the club during any part of their swing. Because the skills they require come naturally, leading to a classic swing, they tend not to need to hit a large number of balls in practice to get positive results on the course. Carlos Franco, another excellent example of a Classic Swinger, is a multiple winner on tour though he rarely ever hits practice balls. Vijay Singh, known for practicing hard, is a clear exception to this rule!

As a Classic Swinger, you have good tempo—that is, you swing with a faster cadence than the average golfer, though the swing actually *looks* slower to most people. Based on tempo, rhythm, balance, and timing, you use all body parts equally in creating centrifugal force to power your swing. You don't attack the ball as many players ("hitters" of the ball) do. Rather, you swing the club easily through the ball.

As a physically advantaged player you remain in balance through the motion of your golf swing, which is why your swing looks so easy and fluid. Your transition from backswing to downswing is very smooth, which is why it seems as though you hesitate or even stop the club at the top (sometimes called a "gathering motion") before bringing it back down and through the ball.

There is a bit—though not much—of a lateral slide on the downswing of Classic Swingers as they move into the impact position. Nothing in the swing is overdone. Smooth tempo and balance take priority over the hands as a power source. Loren Roberts, a student of mine, is an example of an arms-dominant player whose swing is not built around his hands as a power source. Loren uses those parts of his body that create his most natural method of squaring the blade. He doesn't force anything in his swing. Like all Classic Swingers, Loren maintains a balanced swinging motion while all parts of his body work as one unit.

The Modern Swing shares several characteristics with the Classic Swing, including a reliance on tempo and timing. The difference is primarily in the use of coiling the shoulders against the hips. Typically the Modern Swinger has a 100-degree shoulder turn and only a 30-degree hip turn. The lower body starts the downswing before the upper body has completed its full turn. Generally speaking, the Modern Swing has less motion in it and generates power by using the big muscles of the body.

In the takeaway of the Modern Swinger, the wrists set early and the club stays in front of the chest. The backswing looks like it's about three-quarters compared to the Classic Swing. And like the Classic Swing, there is also a slight lateral slide toward the target during the downswing. Hips and shoulders are open at impact. You'll see the differences between the Modern and Classic Swing more clearly with the swing sequences in chapter 6.

If you're like most players, you probably like the idea of falling into the category of Classic Swinger or Modern Swinger. To see if you truly belong here, try taking the balance test, the eye–hand coordination test, and the body control test.

Balance Test

This test assesses your balance when swinging the club. First find (or cut) two pieces of wood 2 inches (5 centimeters) high by 4 inches (10 centimeters) wide and stack one on top of the other. Standing on top of the boards, start your swing at the finish position, then swing to the start position, and then swing back to the finish position and hold for five seconds. As you swing back, lift your left foot completely off the ground. All your weight will be on your right foot at the top. Now step down with your left foot and hold your balance for five seconds at the finish position.

If you can complete this test without falling off the boards, you have great balance throughout the swing.

Eye–Hand Coordination Test

Generally speaking, you require good eye–hand coordination to excel at golf. Try this little test, which you've probably seen Tiger Woods do on TV in a

Nike commercial. Simply hold your sand wedge with your normal grip and bounce a golf ball on the face of the club (see figure 5.9). How many times can you bounce the ball before missing? If you can bounce it more than 10 times, your eye–hand coordination is excellent. You might well belong in the category of Classic Swinger or even Modern Swinger.

Body Control Test

To judge your general coordination and body control, try this basic arm and leg test. Stand up straight and lift your left leg a few inches or centimeters off the ground (see figure 5.10). Now move your left leg and left arm backward and forward at the same time. Repeat the movement on the right side. If you can maintain balance and control while swinging your arms and legs, you have very good kinesthetic awareness.

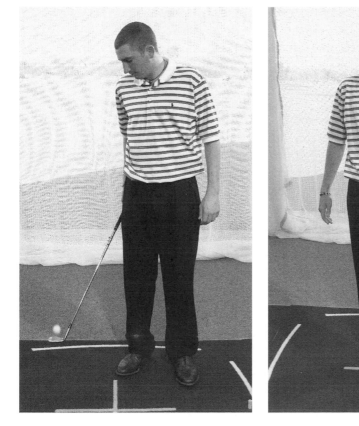

Figure 5.9 Eye–hand coordination test.   **Figure 5.10** Body control test.

Ted Tryba's Swing: Finding His Power Source

PGA player Ted Tryba came to me for some help, telling me he had been advised to swing the club around his body deeper and on a somewhat flatter swing plane than he had been swinging. I knew immediately that in swinging this way Ted would violate his natural power source. Ted has relatively short arms and long legs. He's tight in the chest and doesn't have above-average upper body flexibility to swing the club fully around his body. He also has large, strong hands, making him a natural hands player. To help him with his swing and counter the advice he'd received, I recommended that he swing the club more vertically to take advantage of the natural high arc of his swing. He made the adjustments necessary and began consistently hitting solid shots with optimal power and accuracy.

What's Your Power Source?

After reviewing the four dominant power sources and performing some of the tests, you should have a good idea of where you fit. Now that you've determined your power source, don't make the mistake of trying to change it or of copying a swing that doesn't match your source—that's the biggest mistake you could make. If you're a hands player, you'll never be able to swing like Tiger Woods. Recognize and accept that. You'll still be able to build an excellent swing that's reliable under pressure and that can be modified (*not* changed to another category) if things go wrong.

In chapter 6, I'll give you examples of professional players with swings that use one of the four power sources we've discussed. It's enjoyable to watch players you can pattern your game after, and you can learn a great deal about what you should be doing to develop your own perfect swing.

6

The Pro Swing Model

You should now have a good idea from which source you derive your dominant power: your lower body, upper body, hands, or your natural gifts of rhythm, timing, and balance. In this chapter I'll further refine the four categories, and soon you'll be able to model your swing after a pro golfer on the tour. Many players attempt to imitate the pros but fail because they pick the wrong player. In this chapter, I'll help you pick the perfect player to model your swing after.

Once you have determined your most likely dominant power source, there are four further criteria to look at when selecting a pro model:

1. Physical characteristics—size, strength, flexibility, age, lever length (length of arms, legs, hands, etc.), body type, amount of body fat, and muscularity. All bodies are different, but try to match up as closely as possible with a swing model that looks like you.
2. Preferred ball flight—primarily a draw, fade, or straight pattern. Match up with a pro whose flight matches your goal shot pattern.
3. Grip and stance characteristics—weak or strong grip, wide or narrow stance, closed or open stance, weight left or weight right, ball forward or ball back.

4. Mechanical adjustments—players within each group tend to compensate for certain aspects of their swing by making adjustments in their swing mechanics. You'll want to observe and consider your model's mechanical adjustments and try to adopt them if you think they'll help your ball flight.

Like all players, tour pros can be categorized into the four types of dominant physical power sources. They are upper body players, lower body players, hands players, or Classic Swingers. Let's look at each of the types again, this time while considering the criteria of physical characteristics, preferred ball flight, grip and stance characteristics, and mechanical adjustments. I'll reserve the Modern Swing to the end of this chapter to give us examples of mechanical power sources.

Craig Stadler, Duffy Waldorf, Laura Davies, Bruce Lietzke, Hal Sutton (see figure 6.1), Ed Dougherty (figure 6.2), and Brandie Burton (figure 6.3) are among the many upper body players you might have watched over the years. These players tend to be powerful hitters, not swingers who specialize in using the big muscles of the upper body to square the clubface. If you're trying to determine whether a particular player is an upper body player, look for a square, slightly closed stance. These players also tend to cut the ball and work it from left to right.

Figure 6.1

Hal Sutton addresses the ball. Note the flared feet to help him turn.	The takeaway is very wide and extended, which creates his high swing at the top.	Most upper body players do not extend their arms this much and keep them a little closer to their body than Hal is showing here.

Note the late wrist set on the backswing.	Hal's swing at the top finds both feet on the ground, with very stable legs.	Again, both feet are on the ground at impact, which is a fundamental for the upper body player. This allows the upper body to turn around the legs.	Hal finishes very straight and erect, with his head positioning over his left hip.

Figure 6.2

Champions Tour member Ed Dougherty demonstates his short swing. Notice the amount of forward bend.

Ed sets the club early.

The upper body player allows the elbow to separate at the top.

The upper body provides the power through impact.

Figure 6.3

LPGA player Brandie Burton starts back with the big muscles of the shoulders.

The arms and shoulders take the club back.

Note the club cocking up as her hips and shoulders turn away together.

The shoulders have made a full turn, while the hips have turned half as far. The left foot stays on the ground.

Ed uses the one-piece takeaway typical of the upper body player.

An early set of the right shoulder and wrists seems to add leverage in the upper body swing.

Ed's lack of flexibility doesn't allow him to get a full turn.

Brandie keeps her wrists cocked until the last minute to get her power.

The head is behind the ball at impact.

Brandie's hands, arms, and upper body release and provide the power.

Physical Characteristics

Upper body players share the following physical characteristics:

- Large upper body and torso; wider than average shoulders
- Short arms and short overall height, typically 64 to 68 inches (162-172 centimeters)
- Below average upper body flexibility
- Reliance on upper body strength and muscle power (rather than a long swing with high centrifugal force) to produce clubhead speed

Ball Flight Pattern

Both Craig Stadler's and Craig Parry's (figure 6.4) ball flight patterns are typical of upper body players in that they work the ball left to right. Because of the upper body player's physical makeup and swing characteristics, they tend to cut the ball. Because they are so dominant with the upper body, these players hang on through impact, which means the back of the left hand is further out in front of the club than normal, and the hand remains in that position longer through impact. If they didn't hold on through impact, these players would be hitting some really ugly hooks.

Figure 6.4 Craig Parry, an upper body player, *(a)* shows his flying right elbow at the top of his swing and *(b)* his over-the-top downswing. Most upper body players line up in a closed stance, take the club back inside and around their bodies on the backswing, and swing across their body line through impact.

Stance and Setup

Most upper body players swing from a square to slightly closed stance. However, you see more than a neutral amount of upper body tilt in the setup and backswing of these players. They tend to tilt their spine more away from the target at setup because of their strong grip. They bend forward at the hips more than the average swinger so that their arms have room to get by their body. Their grips tend to be strong in the left hand (turned to the right) and neutral in the right hand. Their ball position is somewhat back in their stance. They flare out both feet to make it easier to turn.

The grip position for upper body players is stronger than neutral, and their right-hand grip is in the fingers more than neutral. This grip allows for an earlier set of the wrists and more cocking of the wrists in the backswing. You can't cock from a weak grip nearly as much as from a strong one. By *weak* here I'm still referring to the position of the hands on the club, not to a lack of strength, as much of this category's power comes from strong hands and arms (review chapter 3 for more on grips). In this case *strong* means turning your hands to the right and not to the left.

Swing Mechanics

Most upper body players share a degree of these mechanical adjustments:

- They tend to be hitters, not swingers. They usually employ short, low swings (rather than long, high, fluid swings) that accelerate quickly toward impact.
- They tend to be right-side dominant. That is, more force comes from the right side of their body (for right-handed players) than from their left.
- They tend to set the club early and keep the club in front of their body. Their club is very wide at the top (see Hal Sutton's position on page 127).
- They often have flying right elbows at the top.
- They tend to take narrow, closed stances (because of limited flexibility).
- They tend to fade the ball because of their ever-so-slight outside-in downswing and blocking motion through impact.
- They tend to flare out both feet at address to ease their turn (because of limited flexibility). The head often moves to increase shoulder turn on the backswing.
- The spine tends to tilt backward (away from the target) on the downswing more so than for most players. The tilt allows them to tuck their right arm in front of their upper body.
- The left foot remains on the ground on the backswing. At impact, feet are still on the ground, but the torso is slightly open.
- There's usually small release through impact. They tend to hang on and have long left arms after impact to keep the face open.
- They tend to finish in an erect I position.

Figure 6.5 Duffy Waldorf keeps the club in front of his body.

Figure 6.6 Craig Parry swings over his body line on the downswing. This is a distinctive move of the very inflexible upper body player.

Backswing

One thing you'll notice about upper body players is how relatively short their backswings arc. Although they take only about a three-fourths backswing, they make up for it by accelerating back down to the ball with strength. Even with a shorter backswing, they have a fairly complete shoulder turn, so they get pretty close to 90 degrees in their shoulder turn. This is aided by their closed stance. They keep their arms and club in front of the body through the swing (figure 6.5), which is a fundamental for all swing categories. As an upper body player, you can't afford to get your arms back behind your body and still make the proper rotation through the ball.

Because of a relatively short backswing, upper body players also naturally set the club earlier in the swing and produce a narrow takeaway in the process. Look closely, and you'll see them folding the right elbow into the body on the way up.

Downswing

I often refer to upper body players as *right-side hitters*. Because they use the strength and size of their upper bodies as a dominant power source, they tend to hit against their left sides rather than swinging through the shot. This hitting style is easy to pick out while observing their swings. On the downswing, you can watch the shoulders work out and around on the first part of the downswing. As the downswing proceeds, the right shoulder goes down and under as the right elbow will be on the right hip at impact. This allows the body to square the blade at impact (figure 6.6). This tilt is more dramatic with upper body golfers than any other, although all players make this move to some degree. The swings of upper body players are easy to pick out of a crowd because of a slowing down of the follow-through after impact. Their follow-throughs are shorter than normal because of hitting against their left side. Most of their power is expended at impact rather than through to the finish. This is very pronounced in the swings of all upper body players.

Upper body players such as Bruce Lietzke tend to come over the top of their shoulder line on the downswing. They must do this to keep the club and arms in front of the body. Remember that when I say *over the top*, I mean they swing over the top of the body line, not over the top of the target line. Because they play from a closed stance, they swing outside in over the body line and still square the blade through impact.

Takeaway and Downswing

As I've mentioned, the upper body player tends to set the club early and keep the club in front of the chest. Most golfers who set the club early use only their arms and end up not turning their shoulders. You must turn your shoulder on the backswing to create the width at the top. If you don't, the common result is a casting out with the hands and arms. Better players avoid casting by dropping the right shoulder down as the lower body leads the downswing. On the downswing the right elbow moves very tightly into the right side. This retains the left arm–clubshaft angle during the downswing. Generally speaking, the more acute the left arm–clubshaft angle, the greater the power. At impact, we're looking for the hands to be ahead of the clubhead, which creates the best compression of the ball for the upper body player (see figure 6.7).

Figure 6.7 Duffy Waldorf, an upper body player, tucks his right elbow as his hands stay ahead of his clubhead.

This is a powerful way to play your irons. Sometimes, however, this left-arm–clubshaft angle gets too narrow for the amateur to control. But, it's a good goal because the average amateur tends to cast the club and uncock the wrists early from the top.

Looping the Club

Some upper body players very noticeably appear to loop the club. When I say *loop the club,* I'm referring to a noticeable over-the-top move that appears as if the golfer is coming down outside the way he or she went back. This is common among some upper body players because of their closed stance, their inside takeaway, and their large upper body. Craig Stadler is a good example. Craig sets up slightly to the right of the target in a closed stance. He then takes the club slightly inside and around his body until he gets the club to the top. Then he starts down by rotating his upper body ever so slightly from the top. This makes his swing look like he's looping to the outside or over the top. He then drops his right shoulder straight down and tucks his elbow to his side. This gets the club back on the correct inside path. The appearance is that the swing is coming over the top, but it's actually only coming over the stance line. Other players who swing with this outside loop are Craig Parry, Bruce Lietzke, Larry Nelson, and Hale Irwin. All these players play a left-to-right shot.

Short Versus Long Swingers

Within the upper body category, there are short and long swingers. Craig Stadler is an example of a short swinger; I've already talked about the three-fourths length backswing. Many Champions Tour players have short swings. If you're an upper body player and lack strength or control, use an earlier wrist set (see chapter 7 for information).

Some upper body players on the PGA Tour are longer swingers, such as Hal Sutton and Peter Jacobsen. These players use more of a sweeping motion on their downswing and tend to be very good drivers of the ball. They can't get their power with a shorter swing, so they get their arms a little higher at the top of the swing. This sweeping motion also contributes to better than average wedge play.

Long swingers are similar to other upper body players, though they do differ in a few ways. The swings of long swingers look fuller because of a longer backswing. They have a more extended takeaway, which extends the width of their arc. They generally have longer and higher finishes. They tend to get more height at the top of their swing. Players such as Hal Sutton and Raymond Floyd want greater height at the top of their swings, so they let the right elbow "fly" or separate on the backswing, which is fine as long as it reconnects on the downswing. This elbow position also opens up the clubface at the top of the swing more. The "flying elbow" is pretty consistent with upper body players with large chests and wide shoulders.

As I've said, upper body players can be either short or long swingers. Hal Sutton told me that he doesn't feel as if his legs get involved in the swing at all. He feels that he rotates his upper body over very quiet legs. I can tell you for certain that Hal's legs *are* involved in his swing, but not to a large extent, and there's almost no slide in his legs. Many other upper body players have Hal's Popeye forearms and wide shoulders. In observing his swing, you'll notice he covers the ball with his body through impact (see figure 6.8), meaning that the right side and chest are well-rotated through impact as the torso opens up. It's as if he's turning his right shoulder down and at the ball. Hal's swing is very right-sided with the torso turning over quiet legs.

Ian Woosnam, another upper body player, gets pretty aggressive with his body on the downswing. He finishes in an erect and balanced I position with his head directly over his front leg (see figure 6.9).

Figure 6.8 Hal Sutton covers the ball and aggressively opens his chest at impact.

Figure 6.9 The I finish of upper body player Ian Woosnam. All upper body players finish this way.

Jack Nicklaus brought the use of the legs to the forefront of golf. Because he was the dominant player of his era, many golfers tried to emulate his swing and leg drive. He played in the lower body category for a long time and is still trying to do so, but his flexibility is not at a point at which he can play this way as effectively. It's ironic, because Jack's legs served him so well over a long and very successful career, that it was his leg drive that eventually caused his back and hip problems. There's a lesson senior players can learn from Jack. If you've been a lower body player most of your life, but you begin losing leg strength and flexibility in your hips, it's time to see your local professional and look into changing your swing. When a lower body player experiences hip problems, the power connection with the legs is broken, which is why several tour players (e.g., Greg Norman, Steve Elkington, Jesper Parnevik) have struggled to regain their swing form after hip surgery. Whenever you begin to lose elements of your dominant physical power source, it's time to consider a change in your swing.

You might recognize Nancy Lopez, Betsy King, Patty Sheehan, Juli Inkster (figure 6.10), and many LPGA players as lower body players. Other tour players who fit into this category are Davis Love III, Tiger Woods, Jim Furyk, Phil Mickelson, Jesper Parnevik, and Scott Hoch (figure 6.11 on page 138). Lee Trevino has short legs but has used a leg drive throughout his career.

Figure 6.10

Juli Inkster's setup, showing good posture.

Shoulder and chest take-away.

One-piece takeaway with late wrist set.

The top of Juli's swing shows her high swing with the right elbow flying.

The downswing shows her legs driving down with her weight going into the ground.

Note how the hips open at impact with the right elbow on the right hip, with the right heel up off the ground.

Juli's high finish.

Figure 6.11

PGA Tour player Scott Hoch at setup.

A wide one-piece takeaway with the club in front of the body.

Notice the breaking up of the club and the flying right elbow during the backswing.

Hoch's top-of-the-swing position shows a high swing, a flying right elbow, and an open face, all signatures of the lower body player.

Hoch's legs start his downswing so his right elbow can reconnect to his body.

Aggressive leg action through impact with a very handsy release. Most lower body players hook the ball.

Physical Characteristics

Lower body players share the following physical characteristics:

- Long or powerful legs supplying a great deal of power. The torso is short, the legs are long.
- Longer than normal arms (e.g., Davis Love III)
- Generally, thin chests and narrow shoulders
- Predominant fast hips through impact (particularly in women players)
- Timing, tempo, rhythm, balance, and power all based on footwork

Ball Flight Pattern

You see more draw shots (right to left for right handers) from leg players than from any other pattern. Most hook the ball, but as I've stressed, ball flight patterns are determined in great measure by how these pros set up. Davis Love III goes the opposite way and is a left-to-right player with this power source. Colin Montgomerie lines up to the left of his target and hits a left-to-right shot every time. Fred Couples does the same, and so does Rich Beem. I'm pointing these players out because they're the exception to the rule—most lower body players move the ball right to left. This is a result of a somewhat handsy action through impact coming from the hip slide in their downswing.

Lower body players who drive their hips really hard through the downswing hit the ball more left to right, and that is a key thing to look for in your own ball flight. The more hip action, the more likely you'll produce a left-to-right pattern. When I say hip action, I am referring to opening up the hips. In other words, the more open the hips are at impact, the more likely the ball will fade. If you're seeing a fade in your shots, you're likely driving your hips harder and faster than normal through the downswing.

Generally, more slide in the legs than neutral promotes a hook. I've referred to lateral leg slide several times and want you to understand that, for lower body players, the higher the swing arc gets at the top of the backswing, the more slide there must be in order to reconnect the arms with the body and to square the blade at impact. This category of golfer typically squares the blade through leg action. Tom Lehman is a good example of a lower body player who slides his lower body a lot and hits a hook.

Stance and Setup

Most, though not all, lower body golfers use neutral to weak grips. You'll see these players standing more erect and closer to the ball in their setup. Look at figure 6.12 of Davis Love III to see what I mean. Davis stands more erect because of his height. He can stand closer to the ball because, though he's tall, he's also thin in the chest, so his hands can hang down straighter to the club. The stances of lower body players are generally closed and wide. Their ball position tends to be more forward than most players to accommodate their high swing plane and aggressive movement to the left side.

The way you set up to the ball is very important to the outcome of your swing. Players who set up more open to the target—such as Fred Couples, Mark Calcavecchia, and Colin Montgomerie—have wider and higher backswings, rotate more aggressively through the ball, swing outside to inside through impact, and produce a slight cut in their swings, thus producing the left-to-right ball flight pattern mentioned earlier. Players setting up in more of a closed position with this power source, such as Dan Forsman, are still wide and high on the backswing, but they produce additional leg slide in the downswing, are less open with their hips at impact, and thus hit hooks. These players also position the ball slightly more back in their stances.

The stance of lower body players tends to be wider to support their higher swings. There are always exceptions to the rule, and one of them is Scott Hoch, who has a narrower stance than most players in this category. Scott was told many times that he was too leggy in his swing, so some time ago he narrowed his stance. He now has an unusually narrow stance for such a high swing. This eliminates his excessive leg slide.

How wide your stance should be depends largely on how flexible you are. Players who don't want a lot of slide in their legs tend to narrow their stance. A wider stance helps the lower body player keep the legs more

Figure 6.12 Lower body players who have thin chests like Davis Love III tend to stand closer to the ball in order to block excessive arm swing. This posture tends to allow the lower body player to turn his shoulder relatively level to the ground while his arms swing very high.

stable on the backswing and more leggy on the downswing. The right foot is usually straight in the setup, with the left foot flared out slightly toward the target.

Generally, the ball position for the lower body player is well forward. This is because the leg drive on the downswing moves the hips some four to six inches (15 centimeters) farther forward at impact than they were at address (see figure 6.13). This center of gravity movement forward requires the ball position to be more forward than usual. So, if you feel you have very aggressive leg action, try putting the ball more forward. Jack Nicklaus often advocated this ball-forward position for all clubs. Byron Nelson did the same. Both had high swings and aggressive leg action.

a **b**

Figure 6.13 *(a and b)* Jeff Sluman gets his power from his wide backswing and his fast lower body rotation.

The basic ball positions for the lower body player are

- off the outside edge of the shoulder for the driver,
- under the armpit for fairway woods (and longer irons up to 6-iron), and
- under the logo of the shirt for short iron shots (that is, halfway between the sternum and the armpit when the left arm is at the side of the body).

Swing Mechanics

Most lower body players share a degree of the following mechanical adjustments to their swings:

- They tend to maintain a very straight right arm within a one-piece takeaway controlled by their shoulders and chest.
- Their right arm tends to be above their left arm on the takeaway.
- Their hips are usually open or facing the target at impact.
- Their left foot tends to come off the ground during the backswing. (Note that Jack Nicklaus *allowed* his left foot to come off the ground in response to the pull of his body. Jack let the momentum of his swing bring the foot up; he never *forced* his foot up, as I see many amateurs doing.)
- They have a bigger hip turn on the backswing than most swing styles (this depends largely on degree of flexibility).

Figure 6.14 Steve Lowery, a lower body player, shows his reverse C finish that results from his tremendous leg drive on the downswing. This is very hard on the back. Also, notice how much his legs have moved laterally toward the target.

- They tend to maintain a very centered and steady head but allow their heads to rotate to the right on the backswing.
- They tend to use a 90-degree or more shoulder turn on the backswing, as well as quite a bit of hip turn. (Fred Couples is an exception in that he has less hip turn, but more coil, in his backswing and more active legs going down. Fred drives his hips through the ball very hard and fast. It's only his hip turn on the backswing that differs. Note that Fred is another lower body player with chronic back problems.)
- Their hips tend to be open 45 degrees to the target at impact (see Jesper Parnevik's swing style).
- They are generally very athletic and have a great deal of eye–hand coordination (because this is a high-maintenance swing).

- Most junior golfers and women in this category have leggy swings because their legs are normally the strongest part of their bodies.
- They have a high swing and a reverse C finish (see figure 6.14).

Backswing

Lower body players tend to keep their heads very still. They have to because their high swings and big arcs demand a steady center for better control (see figure 6.15). The fundamental I apply is that the head must stay inside the feet for the best result. Any movement off the ball to the right makes the lower body player very inaccurate.

The backswing arc tends to be very wide with a late wrist set. The takeaway is performed with the big muscles of the shoulders and chest and is often called a one-piece takeaway. This wide takeaway drives the club up into a high position. Generally, the lower body player gets the body turn over very early and then lifts the arms high above the head.

a   b

Figure 6.15 *(a)* Dan Forsman and *(b)* K.J. Choi show their high swing arcs that help them with their distance.

A Free Hip Turn

Generally, the hips of the lower body player turn freely on both the backswing and forward swing. There are no restrictions. Again, take Jack Nicklaus as an example. The hips turn freely on the backswing and seem to turn more than the modern swing suggests. The left heel might come off the ground. The hips turn at least 45 degrees on the backswing, and the right hip is always positioned inside the right heel when the swing reaches the top. This means that the right leg must act as a post to turn against. This is a fundamental for all swings to adhere to.

The Top of the Swing

Just as no one swing fits all, there's no one position at the top that is common to all lower body players. There are only tendencies. For example, most lower body players have high, long, "lazy" swings (figure 6.16) like Davis Love III's. But there are some lower body players with very short swings and fast, quick leg action, such as Lee Trevino. In either case, the timing and power for the swing comes from the lower body.

Some lower body players have such big turns and high swings that their club points across the target line at the top of the swing. This is caused by the "flying" right elbow characteristic of the high-swinging lower body player.

Figure 6.16 Davis Love III gets his club high at the top to maximize his power.

Four Turns on the Backswing

The lower body player has four distinct turns on the backswing: in the shoulders, the hips, the knees, and the head. The head and knees don't turn much—just enough for the golfer to get a free body turn (see figure 6.17). If the head and knees stayed still, the golfer wouldn't be able to get behind the ball.

Downswing

The downswing of the lower body player is driven by his or her dominant power source, the legs. Typically, the higher the swing, the more the legs must slide toward the target in the downswing for the arms to reconnect with the body. The legs slide first and then rotate during the downswing. Swing positions tend to be wide on the takeaway and high at the top (see figure 6.18); the slide occurs to reconnect the arms, and then there's the rotation. Because of this action, lower body players swing from inside the body line and are very active with their hands through impact. The high-swinging lower body players tend to be quite handsy through impact, with an inside-out path through the ball. In most cases, this creates a hooking action.

Figure 6.17 Billy Mayfair shows his one-piece takeaway with a late wrist set and a free hip turn.

Figure 6.18 Juli Inkster's wide, high swing, showing an open face.

With higher swings, in which the legs do much of the work on the downswing, the hands tend to get "wristy" through impact (that is, there's more wrist action than normal). Lower body players, because of their leg drive, finish with their bodies bowed back in the shape of a reverse C, their hands very high (see figure 6.19).

They are so inside out on the downswing that the hands are forced up higher in the finish. If you're attempting to imitate this swing, be forewarned that players pushing their back this hard and aggressively into the reverse C position usually end up with back problems. Tiger Woods, Colin Montgomerie, and Jim Furyk play this way. The harder the leg drive, the bigger the reverse C at the finish.

Figure 6.19 Juli Inkster's high finish. The finish is usually a mirror image of the top of the swing position.

Takeaway

In lower body players you typically see wider, one-piece takeaways (see figure 6.17). They use their shoulders for the takeaway and set the club later in the backswing, which drives the club up higher at the top. Because of the long, high swing arc, the right elbow might "fly" a little bit on the way up, and the club might cross the line at the top. Look for this motion in the swings of Fred Couples and John Daly. These guys are very leggy, have wide and high swing arcs, and let the right elbow fly. The clubface tends to be very open in a vertical position at the top of the swing because of the height of the swing arc (see figure 6.18). Keep looking at clubface positions—you can usually get a read on them even in the fastest of swings. Watch how their downswings tend to loop or rotate to the inside. This reconnects their arms to their body and prepares them for a powerful inside-out hit.

Players with powerful forearms and hands typically use the hands to square the clubface (see figure 6.20). In our age of trying to put everybody into a modern swing with a lot of body action and passive hands, we've done an injustice to the player who has fast, sensitive, and strong hands. Before the use of video cameras and great shaft technology, golfers tended to use their hands more than they do now. But eye–hand coordination is the heart and soul of the golf swing.

Figure 6.20

Champions Tour member Hubert Green setup with hands pressed ahead of the ball activates the hands in the takeaway.

Handsy takeaway.

Full and early wrist set.

Top of swing shows very little turn and arms close to the body.

Wrists cock even more on the downswing.

Hands are ahead of clubhead at preimpact, a mark of all good strikers.

Hubert's position at impact includes a flat left wrist and bent right wrist.

If this is music to your ears, take heart because you don't have to swing like Tiger Woods to be a consistent, effective player. Use your strengths, not your weaknesses. If you think you're a hands player, then go ahead and try taking full advantage of your hands. Play the hands game and see how it works for you. One thing to watch out for—because their hands are busy squaring the blade at impact, hands players tend to hook the ball. Dana Quigley, a very successful Champions Tour member, uses a short swing and a blocking motion with his hands to control the ball (see figure 6.21). Although he is not releasing the club with his hands, he is still using them to square the clubface by holding off the hook with his strong hands.

Figure 6.21

Dana Quigley's setup position.

Note that his takeaway is wide and extended.

The top of the swing shows a flat and short swing for a tall man. This is the signature for a hands player.

Note how the wrists cock even more at the start of the down-swing.

Impact with sliding leg action, which creates a blocking release with the hands. Tall golfers with long legs tend to slide.

Because he's well known and typifies this category, I encourage hands players to watch the style of Seve Ballesteros in his prime and learn from it. Other prominent hands players include Isao Aoki, Hubert Green (figure 6.20), Chi Chi Rodriguez, Lanny Wadkins, Dave Barr, and José Maria Olazabal. Most of these players are on the Champions Tour. As I mentioned, this style of play is not trendy right now, so you don't see many younger golfers playing the hands game (which is a shame because it's the natural style for many players). Looking at players on the tour, Corey Pavin is one player with many attributes of the typical hands player. He's mostly arms, but he gets pretty aggressive with his hands at the bottom of his swing.

Because hands players are probably the toughest for many people to distinguish just by watching them, I'll go into more detail in my general comments before discussing physical characteristics and specific elements of the swing. Keep in mind that these comments are general and don't apply to every hands player; still, this information should help develop your eye for what to watch for when you're trying to spot a hands player.

In general, hands players need to consciously speed up or slow down their hands and arms to stay in sync with their body during their swing. Their athleticism allows them to play with a few compensations in their swing. They have primarily fast-twitch muscle fiber in their musculature, which allows most of them to be "hitters" and not "swingers" of the club. For example, most would consider a guy like Dana Quigley (figure 6.21), who is very tall and thin with long arms and legs, a hands player. But, more generally, golfers like Allen Doyle, D.A. Weibring, and John Bland fit the mold of the typical hands player.

The swings of the hands players often look unconventional or creative. These players tend to be short hitters but hit generally very straight. They are known as shot makers because of their ability to work the ball right or left. They tend to be great around the green because of their ability to control the clubhead with their hands.

As you'd expect, the bodies of hands players are typically the secondary power source in their swings. Although most players in this category say they don't put much leg action into their swings, all swings involve the legs to some degree. It's true you don't usually see much slide in the legs; typically, they swing their hands and arms over stable legs. With a lot of hand and arm rotation, hands players tend to open and close the clubface a lot.

Here's an interesting bit of information for you. Although most hands players are quite flexible, many golfers become hands players because they lose flexibility in their bodies and need the added power from their hands. If you play with other power sources and find them seriously eroding, you might want to ask your instructor if you should consider the hands style of play.

Now, before giving the specifics of players in this category, let me say there's a lot of variation among hands players; you're apt to see about anything in their homemade swings. I mean this in a good way—these players are demonstrating their creativity and shot-making abilities.

Physical Characteristics

No one body build fits all hands players, so it's difficult to categorize these players according to their physical characteristics. Sometimes their body build and their physical characteristics have little or nothing to do with their hands-dominant style. Still, some generalizations can be made. Many hands players share the physical attributes listed here:

- Large, strong, sensitive hands with longer fingers, allowing them to feel the position of the clubhead through the entire swing
- Very flexible wrists
- Quick reflexes
- Great coordination and balance; tend to be very athletic
- Tend to be muscular

Ball Flight Pattern

Most hands players hook the ball as they tend to be on their right side at impact. You don't see many cutters (slicers) among hands players. Because they don't use their bodies as much, they're not extremely long with their shots. What they lose in distance, they try to make up in creativity. For one reason or another, early in their careers most of these players were forced to create a lot of shots. Many hands players learned the game with only a few clubs and played in places where they had to create shots; they are the true shot makers of the game. Personally, I think their swings reflect the conditions they grew up playing in and the limitations of their equipment and the geography they grew up in. They learned to do their best with what they had.

As I mentioned, there aren't a lot of hands players left, especially on the regular tour. You're going to find that most of the younger players are proponents of the Modern Swing.

Stance and Setup

Hands players prefer weaker grip positions so they can manipulate the clubface more through the swing. Their grips are also a little more in the palms than neutral. With a weaker grip position, they can open and close the clubface more than the average player through the swing. Consequently, they sense the action of the clubhead more than other players. Many of them talk about being "feel" players. I think that many women golfers have the necessary feel or touch to be hands players, but they usually lack the strength they need in their hands and arms, so they're not often included in this category.

I've talked about the setup as the most controllable part of the game. It's also the most observable as you watch the professional of your choice. One of the things you'll see in their setup is a lower handset position (see figure 6.22). They position their hands in this manner to set the club much earlier in the backswing.

Isao Aoki is a player who uses this lower hand position, and you'll see it in many other Champions Tour players as well. You can spot them pretty easily out on the practice tee by their low handset and the extra forward bend in their postures. When I talk about the golf swing being an eye–hand coordination game, I'm referring especially to the hands player.

The weaker grip of the hands player makes them rely on their hands and arms for squaring the face. They tend to set up more centered over the ball rather than behind the ball. They generally move the ball around in their stance to fit the shot, but their overall tendency is to play the ball more forward in their stance. Their stance is generally narrow and tends

Figure 6.22 The low position of the hands player at address allows the hands player to set his hands immediately.

to be closed for the driver. Their postures are usually more bent over from the hips to accommodate their low hands at address. If their legs are overly active, they'll likely hit the ball to the right.

Swing Mechanics

Most hands players share a degree of the following mechanical adjustments to their swings:

- Hands players tend to rely on their hands for their acceleration through the ball at impact, and they square the blade with the hands as well.

- The top of the swing is generally short and flat, with a quick tempo. The clubface is usually open faced at the top, with the club "laid off" to the left.

- Their swings are usually flat and low; they move from the inside out through the hitting area. Look for low, flat back swings as well as flat finishes

- Most of these players are total "feel" players, so watch for shot making and creativity.

Takeaway

Hands players load the club with their hands right away, which means they set the club almost immediately on takeaway. Players with a low hand position have more bend at the waist. They load the club with their hands, wrists, and elbows and then turn their bodies. Because of their weak grip position, they don't have as much turn in their bodies as other players. Their swings are lower and flatter, with more arm action and less body motion. Because these players are generally blessed with above average coordination, they can spin the ball almost at will.

Downswing

Through the downswing, their body movement causes a distinctive inside loop on the downswing. Hands players tend to either hang back on the downswing or get on top of the ball with their upper bodies. Thus, they don't swing through the shot as an upper body player would. As a result, their weight is about 50-50 at impact, and their upper body is over, or behind, the ball. This produces a very short, but very connected, release. Because they use their hands so much that the hands swing around the body, they generally finish flat or left of the target. Often, their downswing looks very narrow as they load the club more on the downswing.

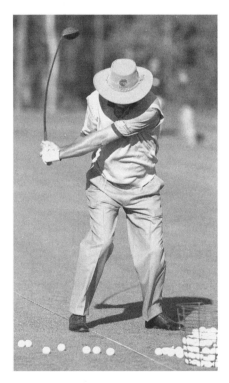

Figure 6.23 Hubert Green, a hands player, shows his left arm–clubshaft angle on the downswing.

As you'd expect, hand speed is very important to hands players, which is why they set the club early, retain the set on the downswing, release through impact, and reset the hands on the follow-through. This produces a lot of rotary action with the body. Their handset on the follow-through is a mirror image of the handset on the backswing.

Impact

The hands player usually has a bowed left wrist at impact (see figure 3.20a on page 48), which is a direct result of the weak grip. The other wrist position you sometimes see at impact is a slightly cupped left wrist (see figure 3.20b on page 48), which can promote a hooking action usually associated with a stronger grip. This is sometimes called a flip release. José Maria Olazabal plays this way. The hands player gets most of his or her speed from the left arm–clubshaft angle created on the downswing and from the speed of the hands (figure 6.23).

I mentioned earlier that some players fall into multiple categories, as did Payne Stewart. He tended to be a leggy player with a high swing, but he was definitely a Classic Swinger, not a hitter. I always enjoyed watching Payne's effortless swing. Other players in this category are Ben Crenshaw, Loren Roberts (see figure 6.24), Steve Elkington, Phil Mickelson (see figure 6.25), Vijay Singh, Sam Snead, Gary Hallberg, Billy Mayfair, Al Geiberger, Larry

Figure 6.24

Loren Roberts sets up in a relaxed posture with no arm tension.

The arms and shoulders take the club away.

The club sets at 9 o'clock.

The Classic Swinger has a 45-degree hip turn and 90-degree shoulder turn.

Loren's preimpact position shows the club parallel to the target line and in front of the golfer on the downswing.

Loren demonstrates the natural release of the Classic Swinger.

All Classic Swingers have great balance.

Mize, and many of the female players on the LPGA Tour. Bobby Jones was a Classic Swinger. He turned his hips a lot, had a one-piece takeaway, and a very smooth swing. I saw Gary Hallberg's swing when he was coming out of college and still think it's one of the smoothest swings I've ever seen. The Classic Swinger tends to be tempo driven and can be easily identified with no rushed movements in his swing.

Figure 6.25

Phil Mickelson demonstrates the relaxed set-up of the Classic Swinger.

Classic Swingers have a long, flowing takeaway.

Everything is turning fully and together.

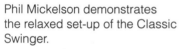

Phil shows the big hip turn and long swing of the Classic Swinger.

The wrists cock even more on the downswing.

The perfect impact has both arms extended with the weight on the front leg.

Some people call Classic Swingers "light hitters," but they're not. Some of them hit the ball a long way, and they're not hitters at all—they're swingers. Any way that you want to say it, they have pretty swings to watch. They are not mechanical looking and tend to have long, flowing swings with good tempo. Quite a few players in this category slow down and gather their swings at the top.

As I mentioned, most professional women golfers fall into this category because of their high, smooth, rhythmic swings. When a player's swing seems effortless, it's pretty certain he or she is a Classic Swinger. Exceptional rhythm and tempo are the hallmarks of their swings. There's no forced or quick motion. These players base their entire motion on rhythm, tempo, and a gradual acceleration of energy. The motion is fluid, with no quick or jerky movements anywhere in the swing.

This category of player balances all the major power sources. They engage the entire body in the production of centrifugal force, which includes using sequential motion as a power accumulator. I've mentioned elsewhere that sequence is timing. If the backswing sequence of the Classic Swinger is (1) clubhead, (2) hands, (3) arms, (4) shoulders, (5) torso, (6) hips, (7) knees, and (8) feet, then their downswing sequence is (1) feet, (2) knees, (3) hips, and so on. Timing, rhythm, tempo, and balance are integral parts of their game. They base everything on centrifugal force and on accumulating power through the entire swing. Their swing looks effortless because it is. There are no fast-moving parts except at impact. They seem to get their power by retaining their left arm–clubshaft angle and allowing centrifugal force to do its job.

Physical Characteristics

Classic swingers share the following physical characteristics:

- Body proportions are balanced.
- The chest is thin and the arms are long.
- The overall look is generally very athletic.
- Generally very flexible.
- Little body fat.

Ball Flight Pattern

I'd say this category has a pattern that's a little bit more right to left, with just slight draws. That said, these players can hit about any shape of shot they want because they have such a high level of touch with, and control over, the clubhead, which is an important element of their swing. Still, every good player should build a single dominant ball flight pattern into his or her game, which is one of my fundamentals. Plus, all good players want to miss shots in only one direction. That may sound negative, but it's not. Golf is not a perfect game, and even the pros miss quite a few shots in a typical golf round. However, their misses are in one direction, allowing them to take half of the trouble out of play.

Stance and Setup

The key word here is *neutral*. The stance is not too wide—about the length of a walking stride. Both feet are flared at address to allow for a free hip turn. These players have three basic ball positions: under the armpit for the driver, under the logo on the shirt for long irons and fairway woods, and underneath the sternum for everything else.

The posture is balanced with a 25-degree bend from the hips forward, and there's only a slight side bend to the right. The Classic Swinger has a neutral, two-knuckle grip, generally with no deviations. The grip is tension free to ensure a smooth swing.

Swing Mechanics

Classic Swingers have a neutral swing with few or no compensations. If it's a beautiful and effortless swing, it's probably the swing of a Classic Swinger. Here are some typical aspects of this swing to look for when you're looking for a model:

- Classic Swingers tend to turn their hips a lot; look for a one-piece takeaway and an extremely smooth swing.
- They base their motion on rhythm, tempo, and a gradual acceleration of energy. There's no forced motion from the top.
- They engage their entire body in the production of centrifugal force and use sequential motion for power.

Takeaway

Like the stance and grip, the takeaway is also neutral, which means there's some shoulder and chest movement combined with some arm and hand motion. There's not an early set as with the hands player and some upper body players.There's certainly not too much extension, as with the lower body player.

Top of the Swing

There's generally an on-plane motion at the top of the swing. Look for a square position at the top with the left wrist, left forearm, and clubface all lined up parallel to one another (see figure 6.26). The left wrist is generally flat with the right elbow pointed down. From this position, it's hard to make a mistake. Most Classic Swingers have rather big hip turns on the backswing, a trademark of their swing (see figures 6.27 and 6.28).

Figure 6.26 Left wrist, left forearm, and clubface all lined up at the top.

Figure 6.27 Gary Hallberg's tempo is superb. Photos don't do justice to his slow change of direction.

Figure 6.28 Mark O'Meara falls into the Classic Swing style with his wonderful tempo.

Figure 6.29 Larry Nelson, Champions Tour player, epitomizes the Classic Swing style with his slow change of direction.

The Downswing

A very slow and leisurely change of direction from backswing to downswing is the earmark of the Classic Swinger (see figure 6.29). The movement is so smooth it looks almost as if the club is stopping up there (but really it's only slowing down). The arms and body seem to work together on the downswing, but the lower body stays slightly ahead of the upper body as the arms come in close to the body. The approach is neither too inside nor too outside but right on line.

As the player enters impact, centrifugal force starts working, which is what makes the swing look so nice and easy. As in all swings, a flat left wrist and a bent right wrist with hands ahead of the clubhead is the result (see figure 6.30).

Finish

The finish is straight up and down, with the shoulders and torso outturning the hips and the head positioned over the left leg. The knees are touching, the chest is facing left of the target, and the hips are facing the target (see figure 6.31).

Figure 6.30 Ernie El's impact shows complete extension at impact and effortless power.

Figure 6.31 Scott Simpson gets to his left side by getting a straight, balanced finish.

The Modern Swing

As mentioned earlier, the Modern Swing fits the second way to produce power—through mechanical advantage. Even though each person's swing is modified to suit his or her particular physical power source, there are also some mechanical aspects of the Modern Swing that produce power that I will discuss here. The Modern Swing is for the player who has a balanced physical power source—that is, no one part (lower body, upper body, etc.) is stronger than another.

The Modern Swing is not for everyone. It's for the golfer who is athletic, trim, muscular, and flexible. Many amateur and recreational golfers try to copy this style, but it's difficult for them to do, especially with an inflexible or out-of-shape body. The clear advantage of this swing is that it's the most accurate way to strike a golf ball. The swing operates on a single plane, creates incredible coil, and forces the hands to stay passive through the hitting zone. It's a down-the-line swing that can hit the ball either way. It creates maximum distance with minimum movement. What more could you ask?

But there are drawbacks, for one that it's only for the very athletic. Some of you may not be able to accomplish this swing, but the following sections will provide information on its potential.

For a model of the Modern Swing, watch Justin Leonard. He's a little on the high side at the top but still represents the style well. Other players to watch include Ernie Els, Charles Howell III, David Toms, Steve Flesch, David Frost, Nick Faldo, Tiger Woods (see figure 6.32), Beth Daniels (see figure 6.33), Stuart Appleby (see figure 6.34 on page 162) and Chip Beck (see figure 6.35 on page 162).

Figure 6.32

Tiger Woods' setup position—hands under shoulders as shoulders are parallel and left of the target line. Weight is on the balls of the feet in perfect balance.

The Modern Player keeps the club in front of the body during the takeaway.

The top of the swing shows very little hip turn but a tightly coiled upper body. The Modern Swing has a lower, more rounded look. The left arm covers the right shoulder at the top.

Figure 6.33

Beth Daniel's takeaway. Note how the Modern Swinger keeps the club in the front of the body.

The club starts to set as the lower body holds its position.

The clubshaft sets on a steeper plane than the one the shoulders are turning on.

Note how Woods brings the club down with his body, not his arms, a characteristic of the Modern Swing.

The shoulders are still coiled as the club comes down from a slight inside path.

Woods' impact shows a body swing. The hips are open and the shoulders are square as the arms are extended.

The postimpact position shows the tremendous extension of a player with a body swing. Note how the shoulders are catching up to the hips as the right side is aggressively moving through the shot.

The top of the swing. Beth has a short but very efficient swing.

Note how the club comes down on plane with the body, initiating the downswing.

The club is delivered in front of the body.

Beth's impact shows her open body, with her hands following her body to the left. This takes excessive hand action out of the impact area. This is defined as a body release.

Figure 6.34

Stuart Appleby's setup. Note the neutral grip and both feet flared outward.

The takeaway is accomplished more with the arms and less with the shoulders.

The wrists are set when the left arm is parallel with the ground.

Figure 6.35

Chip Beck's balanced setup with weight on the balls of his feet, arms relaxed and hanging, and slightly bent over posture.

Chip shows his sequential takeaway (arms, hands, then shoulders) with the club in front of the hands. Notice the lower body resisting the turn of the torso.

The hands, arms, and clubshaft stay in front of his chest as his shaft is breaking up vertically and on plane.

An on-plane position at the top. The club is pointed down the target line and his torso has coiled against his hips.

The top of the swing requires a tight coil against the resistance of the legs. The swing is short of parallel and connected. Note the wide position of the hands at the top.

The lower body starts the downswing as the shoulders stay back. The downswing is wide.

Note the complete extension past impact, proving that the Modern Player has a body swing.

Chip's downswing shows how the big muscles of his body bring the club down. Note the perfect on-plane position here.

The impact shows how the hips and shoulders are both open, but the hips are a little more open than the torso. Chip's head is still back, and his weight is on the left side

In Chip's release and extension, note the full release of the clubhead as the club moves down the line and arcs back to the inside.

The finish is a result of the body bringing the arms through to a high finish

Figure 6.36 Tom Kite keeps his club in front of his body on the takeaway as he resists with his lower body.

Figure 6.37 Tom Kite keeps his leverage far into the downswing. The lower body is the leader, keeping the wrists cocked far into the downswing.

Dominant Mechanical Power Source

The Modern Swing is a body swing. A strong coil is one of the Modern Swinger's dominant characteristics. Coiling is creating distance through resistance. The Modern Swing is a resistance swing. These players rotate around the spine, turn the upper body against the resistance of the lower body, and create tremendous muscle flex, or coil. The swing is on plane both back and through the ball. It's a mechanically efficient swing and a very accurate, and repeatable, way to swing the club. It's also a more connected swing, with the arms and body working together. The hands and arms stay clearly in front of the body on the backswing (see figure 6.36). The Modern Swing is more of a rounded swing, with the hands finishing far left of the player's head.

These players get much of their power from a tight and centered coil, plus the leverage of the club, but they also create a great deal of leverage power in the backswing by hinging the wrists earlier and folding the right elbow. They maintain this leverage advantage in the downswing (see figure 6.37), then turn hard with the body, keeping the right arm and elbow in front of the body. You can see in figure 6.38 how the arms are in front of the body and the back of the left hand is well ahead of the clubhead impact. This is *not* a leggy, Jack Nicklaus style of swing.

The Modern Swing uses the body, not the hands and arms, to flex the shaft. The hips don't turn much on the backswing, but the shoulders and torso turn a great deal. The club tends to be set a little earlier on the backswing as the right elbow folds, which allows the shaft to stay on a good plane as the right elbow stays in front of the chest. This swing is an extremely centered motion with the coiling of the torso around the spine. The arms at the top tend to be on the low flattish side (see figure 6.39), but this is not true in all cases.

On the downswing, the legs and hips are the leaders, but they aren't emphasized. The body turns over stable legs. The release is called a passive release or a body release because the hands are somewhat passive through the hitting area. This swing is truly a total body swing.

Figure 6.38 Ian Woosnam gets his arms in front of his body prior to impact. This is created by the sequential movement of the body and not by hand and arm manipulation.

Figure 6.39 Stuart Appleby shows the prototypical Modern Swinger's position at the top—low with the left arm covering the right shoulder.

Figure 6.40 Ian Woosnam shows a very on-plane position at the top.

Figure 6.41 Steve Elkington shows the Modern Swinger's arm action on the takeaway. There is a lot of arm swing but very little turn to this point.

Ball Flight

Most Modern Swingers hit the ball straight with little or no curve. Contemporary golf courses, with their narrow fairways and tight greens, are demanding more and more accuracy. However, because of their on-plane swinging motion (see figure 6.40), players with this style can work (draw or fade) the ball equally well.

Setup and Stance

In the stance, both feet flare outward with the stance as wide as a walking stride. Some Modern Swingers play out of an open stance to fade the ball, but you seldom see a closed stance. The knees are pushed out away from one another at address, much like riding a horse.

The grip is neutral to strong but never weak because the Modern Swinger wants to emphasize body action, not arm action. A strong left-hand grip will encourage more body rotation and less hand and arm rotation. The posture is pretty standard, with a 25-degree bend from the hips forward and a slight knee bend. The upper arms rest gently on the chest as the hands and arms are very soft and relaxed. There's also a slight tilt to the right with the spine.

There are three ball positions for the Modern Swinger: the left armpit, the logo on the shirt, and the sternum.

Swing Mechanics

This style player keeps the clubface very neutral all the way back, at the top, and through impact. These players are arm loaders on the takeaway (see figure 6.41), which means they tend to swing their arms, hands, and club into the backswing, and then start turning the shoulders and rotating the body. They do, however, keep the club on plane during this maneuver (see figure 6.42). When I say "arm loader," I mean they're moving their arms initially more than their shoulders. The shoulders turn more in the second part of the swing.

Because of the coiling action of the swing, the angle of the right leg through the shot is very important. Modern Swingers keep their weight more toward the inside of their right heel on the backswing, while shifting their hips over and around the right hip socket. They have to coil back against a strong and well-positioned right leg or else leak a lot of power (see figure 6.43). This creates a better coil because the shoulders and arms stop at the same time at the top rather than the arms running away from the turn, as happens in the swings of many shoulder loaders, such as John Daly and Fred Couples.

Figure 6.42 Jeff Sluman's accurate play is due to his on-plane position at the top. Notice that his left wrist, left arm, and clubface are parallel to one another. Also, notice the angle of his right forearm. It is the same angle as his spine.

Figure 6.43 Chip Beck shows a solid right leg position at the top as he turns around his spine.

This swing is on plane and down the line at impact. Whereas some of the swing types you see are on plane at various points in the shot, the Modern Swinger remains on plane throughout the swing. There's less hand action in the impact area, whereas the more traditional player uses the hands more and swings more inside out on the downswing. The Modern Swing is the straightest, most accurate way to play the game, which is precisely why it has become so popular. These players definitely have a mechanical advantage. They use both torque and leverage to generate power, and by staying on plane they don't dissipate their power through the shot.

You can spot a Modern Swinger's finish from quite a ways off because it's so distinct. Their hands finish more around their bodies and to the left of the target (see figure 6.44). They're turning their torso more around stable legs, thus creating a rounded look. Their finish is much lower than the typical lower body player's high finish (see figure 6.45) and is more rounded at the top.

Figure 6.44 David Duval's rounded finish—a strong characteristic of the Modern Swinger.

Figure 6.45 Dan Forsman, a lower body player, has a high finish.

Summary of the Mechanical Power Sources of the Modern Swing

1. **The left arm to chest connection at impact.** This is one very noticeable mechanical power source in the Modern Swing (see figure 6.46). If the left arm is off the chest at impact, the arms will run off and a push or a hook will result. The left arm to chest connection also forces the body to work with the arms through impact and ensures an inside-to-inside swing path (refer back to figure 2.4 on page 16) through impact.

2. **Little or no lateral movement in the swing.** The straightest drivers have very little lateral (back and forth) movement in the swing. The less lateral the hips are in the downswing, the more accurate a driver you will be. The Modern Swing depends on a good body rotation back and through.

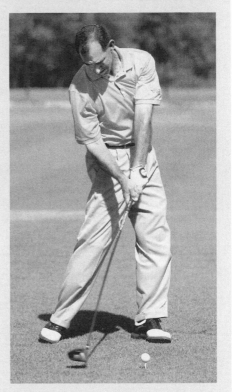

Figure 6.46 The left arm should connect with the chest at impact in the Modern Swing.

3. **Retention of the left arm–clubshaft angle on the downswing.** Because the Modern Swing is such a tight, coiling action around stable legs, the sequence of motion (sometimes called the timing system on the downswing) allows the golfer to maintain the left arm–clubshaft angle far into the downswing. This is called leverage, and it is a major mechanical producer of power (see figure 6.37 on page 164).

4. **Connection.** By connection in the Modern Swing, I mean the distance the arms are from the center or sternum throughout the swing. This distance should be constant and in front of the chest until the golfer reaches the top of the swing, where the club will go in a deep position (see figure 6.39 on page 165).

5. **Rotation.** The Modern Swing gets the majority of its power through a coiling action around stable legs (see figure 6.41 on page 166).

6. **Wrist cock and right elbow fold.** Both the wrist cock and the right-elbow fold provide a certain amount of power for the downswing. Both should be bent around 90 degrees, and the shoulders should also be turned 90 degrees.

7. **Body release.** The Modern Swing uses the body to release the club, not the hands and arms, which accesses more power. It is a body swing in the sense that the body leads it back and the body brings it down.

8. **Torso rotation and closing the gap.** The Modern Swing is a tight, centered, rotary swing that emphasizes the rotation power of the upper torso. The legs are the leaders in the downswing, but the upper body should be trying to catch up and close the gap by impact.

9. **On-plane motion.** The Modern Swing stays on plane all the way through impact, which is why it's such an accurate way to strike the ball (see Chip Beck's position at the top and halfway through the downswing in figure 6.35 on page 162 for examples of this motion).

10. **Sequential motion swing.** The Modern Swing is sequential, and by that I mean everything happens in a linkage system. For example, the backswing order of movement is clubhead, hands, arms, shoulders, torso, hips, knees, and feet. The order of movement is from the ground up in reverse order on the downswing: feet, knees, hips, torso, shoulders, arms, hands, and finally the clubhead. It is this sequential movement that multiplies the power to the next level.

Five Drills for the Modern Swing

The following is a list of the drills for the Modern Swing:

1. Stool-between-the-legs drill. Put a stool between your legs and take only backswings (see figure 6.47). This teaches you to coil your upper body over stable legs as your left shoulder turns behind the ball. This drill quiets the lower legs to produce a better coil. Notice that both feet remain flat on the ground.

2. Towel-under-arms drill. The Modern Swing is a connected swing. When I say "connected," I mean the upper arms stay close to the body and follow the turn both back and through. This drill helps to practice maintaining that connection (see figure 6.48).

3. Club-in-front-of-the-body drill. This drill practices the takeaway for the Modern Swing. Put a club on the ground extending from the left heel running diagonally across the right toe. At the waist-high position, try to get your shaft parallel to the shaft on the ground (see figure 6.49). This keeps the clubhead outside the hands at this point in the swing.

Figure 6.47 Stool-between-the-legs drill. Notice the line from the left shoulder down to the ground. The left shoulder is behind the ball at the top of the swing

Figure 6.48 Towel-under-arms drill.

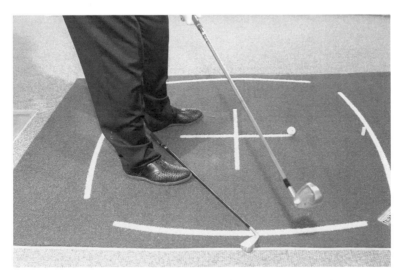

Figure 6.49 Club-in-front-of-the-body drill.

4. Flagstick drill. Use the longest club in your bag or an old flagstick for this drill. Hold the flagstick with your left hand against your left breast, with the stick extending out. Put your right arm on top of the stick. Hold a 7- or 8-iron in your right hand. Now, as you turn back, keep the stick under your right arm (see figure 3.22b on page 49 for a photo of this drill). This keeps the arms and club in front of the body on the backswing, a characteristic of the modern swing.

Figure 6.50 If the club gets "stuck" behind the golfer, a hook or push will result from the inside-outside swing pattern.

5. Pole drill for downswing. The Modern Swing is essentially a body swing with passive hands and a passive release. Sometimes the lower body works so hard on the downswing that the club seems to get stuck too far behind the golfer, which causes hooks and pushes and an overly inside-outside swing pattern (see figure 6.50). To correct this, put a padded golf shaft about one yard behind your ball (see figure 4.20 on page 101). The shaft should be about a 5-iron's length from the ball. Now swing and hit balls while keeping your club on the outside of the shaft on your downswing. This helps the club stay in front of you on the downswing.

We've covered a lot of information in this chapter. At this point, you should have an excellent idea of whether your dominant power source is your upper body, lower body, or your hands. You should know if you qualify to be placed in the group of either Classic Swingers or Modern Swingers. The swing models discussed in this chapter should form the core of your swing—remember that the farther you get from your dominant power source, the more likely it will fail under pressure. In the next chapter you'll learn about customizing your swing and making minor modifications based on personal preference, ball flight, and playing conditions.

Your Customized Swing

Now that you have found—or will soon be looking for—a pro model, the next and last step is fine tuning your swing according to the type of game you want to play. For some players that means adding distance; for others it means altering the ball flight for local or environmental conditions; for still others, it means simply adding in consistency or accuracy. No matter what your swing goals, read each of the sections in this chapter for general information that applies to nearly all golfers and to learn how to modify your swing to come through for you under a variety of circumstances.

Refining the Pro Swing Model

The swing styles you'll find in this section are refinements, or subcategories, of the dominant physical power sources presented in chapters 5 and 6. Many swings have a distinctive flair to them and yet still share a common power source. For example, most of us would easily recognize Arnold Palmer's helicopter finish or Lee Trevino's looping downswing. Nearly every golf swing has its own unique individuality or signature, and, to compound matters, no two golf swings can ever be exactly alike!

In this section I'll present some styles that might look strange at first glance, but if you look closer, you'll see they adhere to the fundamentals of a sound swing. If you have picked a particular pro's swing to model your own swing on, you'll need to discover if your selected pro's swing has any quirks or peculiarities. If so, do they suit your style? If they don't, you need to decide if you still want to model your swing after your chosen pro's swing, quirks and all. For instance, as you learned (or confirmed) in chapter 5, Phil Mickelson, one of the hottest players on the tour, is a Classic Swinger, which means there are a lot of players out there who want to copy his style. But Phil is also what I call a "turner." That is, he has a more prominent than average hip turn in his swing as well as a very long, languid swing. If you have determined that you are a Classic Swinger, and if you have picked Phil's swing to imitate, you need to ask yourself if his prominent hip turn and slow swing suits your style. If it doesn't, then Phil's swing might not be your best choice to use as a model.

So, we'll look at several subcategories in this section, hoping these closer looks help you pick your *best possible* match as you continue to refine your search in the pursuit of your perfect swing. But, remember, even if you believe you have already found your perfect match and you're now anxious to get out on the course and start practicing the new elements of your swing, you should read through the shots, swings, and styles described in the rest of this chapter—you never know when you'll need to pull one of these shots out of your bag.

As you're reading through the following sections, keep some guidelines in mind:

- Always strive for a *realistic* evaluation of the most natural way for you to swing. Don't force things. Don't try to copy someone who has different physical characteristics than you have. Yes, maybe we'd all like to be Classic Swingers, but if we're not, we're not.
- Pick a ball flight and build draw or fade fundamentals into your swing.
- Reduce your arm and hand tension to let yourself swing the way your body will allow you to swing.
- Evaluate swing tempo. If you're a natural fast swinger, keep that style and look for match-ups on the tour. If you're a slower swinger, look for that style. This is important.
- Allow room for your own differences. If you find a swing that you like that's nearly a match but not quite, don't quibble over minor details—give that swing a try. Remember, model your swing after a pro with your same body type and similar flexibility, lever length, and musculature.

Now let's move on to our subcategories of types of swingers. Because we already mentioned turners, we'll start with them.

Turners

You can identify a turner by a big hip turn; a long, slow, deliberate tempo; a long swing; and a somewhat handsy impact. Most turners don't remain centered with their head but rather tend to move their head slightly to the right. They generally have long, high, loose swings that use rhythm and tempo to square up the clubface.

If you have a tight lower body, you may want to consider becoming a turner. Most turners turn significantly on the backswing, slide a little bit toward the target on the forward swing, and then rotate their hips quickly through impact. Another way to pick them out is by their slow change of direction at the top and their leisurely downswing. Most turners also take their front heel off the ground on the backswing. As I've mentioned, Phil Mickelson is

Figure 7.1 Phil Mickelson turns his body to create his long swing.

a definite turner (see figure 7.1). Other players who play (or played) this style are Loren Roberts, Scott Hoch, Larry Mize, the late Payne Stewart, Bobby Jones, Nick Price, Vijay Singh, Billy Mayfair, and Carlos Franco. Most of these players are Classic Swingers, which makes sense because the hip turn is part of what makes the Classic Swing so graceful and pleasant to watch. It is definitely tempo driven. If you have chosen any of these players to model your swing after, ask yourself now if your own swing has a prominent hip turn and flowing motion. If the answer is yes, then you're fine—you have found your model. If the answer is no, then consider selecting as your model another pro from a different style of play.

Coilers

The bottom line is that some players are turners and some are coilers. Whereas turners turn their hips a lot and have slow, long swings, coilers stay centered and coil their upper body around stable legs. Their swing is more of a Modern Swing.

In particular, coilers turn their upper body against the resistance of their lower body. They tend to rotate around their spine with little or no head

Figure 7.2 Ernie Els makes a strong coil. Notice how his left shoulder has turned behind the ball.

movement (see figure 7.2). Coilers have very little hip turn on the backswing but seem to be able to maintain a 90- to 100-degree upper body turn—in other words, you must be very flexible and in top shape to do this. Their swings tend to be very connected and have faster than average tempo. Tiger Woods is a coiler. Other coilers include Ben Hogan, Ernie Els, Len Mattice, Nick Faldo, Robert Allenby, Adam Scott, and Steve Elkington. If your swing resembles the swings of any of these players, you're likely a coiler, too. If you're a coiler, I'd warn against trying to model after a turner, and vice versa.

Pure Rotators

When you stand directly behind players such as Justin Leonard while he's warming up out on the line, the ease with which he rotates around the spine is very easy to pick out. Although Justin's swing is a little on the high side (he has a beautiful Modern Swing), his upper body rotation through the shot is quite noticeable.

Is a draw your natural flight pattern? Are you athletic, with a very flexible torso and hips? If so, you might be a pure rotator. Most pure rotators draw the ball and try to straighten it out a little bit. Notah Begay is a spine rotator who likes to cut the ball, so that's his preferred ball flight. Notah has a rather unusual swing—but I'd still put him into this style group. He has a slightly outside-in path on the downswing and looks as if he covers the ball with his upper body. Plus he has a weak grip and a fast rotating upper body. His grip type has everything to do with his preference of hitting his shots left to right. Sound anything like your game? If your shot goes left to right, have a close look at Notah's swing and style and see if there's anything for you to pick up on.

Rotators tend to have lower, shorter swings and simply rotate around their spine. I call this a one-axis swing because they tend to rotate only around the spine. They are more around than up and down. They square the blade with the rotation of their body. Their swings are simple and have to be very connected (arms on body) to generate the amount of centrifugal force they need because these players release the club with the rotation of their body. As they turn their bodies, the club is going to square up. Fred Funk, who is the straightest driver on the PGA Tour, is a great example of a spine rotator. He simply turns his body to the right and keeps his arms connected to his body on both the backswing and the downswing.

Golfers who rotate around their spine have swing paths that are inside coming down, then go down the target line, and then back to the inside with a low finish. It's a very accurate way to strike a ball because of the minimum amount of hand action needed to play this way. And because their spine doesn't move that much, they create an extremely circular motion with the club.

Figure 7.3 Tom Kite at impact. Notice his rotation of his hips and chest.

Other rotators include Jeff Maggert, who almost won the Masters with his rotating low swing. Chip Beck and Tom Kite (see figure 7.3) are other spine rotators. These players simply rotate on the backswing and rotate again on the forward swing. Generally the pure rotator hooks the ball and his trajectory is low. Additionally, most rotators hit from the inside out. The key is that the body is rotating and not shifting from side to side. If this sounds like your style, watch the rotators I've mentioned closely. Study the swing and then watch your own swing on videotape or in a mirror. Do some comparing and contrasting. If you're seeing more resemblances than not, go with this style and see where it takes you. Find the rotator who matches you best—it might take a little while, but the research should be fun—then try to make that swing your own.

Sliders

There are quite a few hip sliders playing the tour. Curtis Strange won two U.S. Opens with this style. Sliders don't hit their shots quite as far, and they tend to have weak grips, but make no mistake—there are some good sliders on tour, and Curtis is one of the best. My cautionary point to you on sliding versus rotating is that sliders are forced into more compensations in order to square the blade at impact. You already know that one of my key fundamentals is the fewer compensations, the better. The sliding style of play is a two-axis swing, which means that the two hip sockets are the pivot points that the golfer turns his or her upper body around (see figures 7.4 and 7.5).

Jim Colbert and other players with a sliding hip style have a lot of right-side motion through the swing and use more of their muscle power to square the clubface. Leonard Thompson, on the Champions Tour, has a very noticeable slide in both directions. These players are classified as hitters, not swingers, because they use their right sides so aggressively on the downswing to square up the blade. They also must have a very slow body movement in order to control the slide. The disadvantage of being a slider is that you have to get back to where your spine started in order to hit the ball squarely. If your spine moves around a lot you have to have tremendous athletic ability to get back where you started. This makes these golfers rely too much on their hands through impact. The advantage for the average player who is a slider is that this style gives the inflexible body type an easier way to get behind the ball. If you're less flexible than average, you might want to give sliders a good look.

Figure 7.4 Allen Doyle, a successful Champions Tour player, uses a sliding leg action to reduce his hook.

Figure 7.5 The hips and knees slide forward on the downswing.

Tom Lehman is a good example of a slider who draws the ball. It does seem that the longer the golfer's legs are and the higher his or her swing, the more inclined he or she is to slide a little with the legs. So, if you have long legs and tend to be a bit inflexible, this sliding back and forth motion might be good for you. You can't argue with nature. Work with what you've got. If you have longer than average legs, watch sliders and see what you can learn.

Mark McCumber on the Champions Tour has been a "slide blocker" his whole career, and this style seems to work quite well for him. He hits a high, left-to-right fade. You might place Mark Calcavecchia in this group because he slides so much on his downswing. Calcavecchia, however, is more of a slide blocker because as he comes into the ball he slides his hips forward through the shot and then blocks with his hands. "Blocking" means that he extends the left wrist set more through impact than neutral. Mark blocks his hands through impact in order to hit a left-to-right shot. He's also very open at address. He opens up his body way to the left and swings along his open body lines. He has won a lot of tournaments sliding and blocking, so who's to say it's wrong? I say, if it repeats, keep doing it.

Slide blockers tend to have very high swings and are extremely strong in their legs. Slide blockers set up with a very weak grip because they use their right side a lot. They start on their left side, transfer their weight onto their right side, and then slide back over to the left side. Most sliders have very narrow swings at the top. In the process of the downswing, they release the right side as hard as they can to square the blade through impact. The more lateral motion you have in your swing, the earlier you must release the club on the downswing, which is where you might lose some of your power.

High and Low Swingers

Most players who get high at the top of their backswings are very leggy as well. The higher they get in their backswing, the more slide they need to have in their legs to reconnect the arms with the body on the downswing and square the blade back up at impact. The higher they get at the top, the more leg action required to square the blade (see figure 7.6). Fred Couples is a very leggy, high swinger. Other players of this style are Woody Austin, Scott Hoch, Howard Twitty, Jack Nicklaus, Billy Andrade, Davis Love III, Tom Watson, Tom Lehman, Jim Furyk, and Colin Montgomerie. All of these players tend to be very flexible and generally have very handsy releases through impact. If you lack flexibility, this is not the swing for you.

I see more low swingers on the Champions Tour than on any other tour. They probably have low, short swings because they lack the flexibility to get the club up higher, as they could when they were younger. This happens to almost all players as they get older. Even Jack Nicklaus has lowered his swing. Doing so, of course, makes you rely more on hand action through impact in order to square the blade. This is why most low swingers prefer to hook the ball, just as high swingers prefer hitting a fade. You can spot a low swinger by his or her closed stance (aimed to the right) and minimal flexibility. If you have strong hands and are trying to hook the ball, this style is a good one for you. Dave Stockton Sr. demonstrates this type of swing. I'd also put John Bland in this category. Do you swing the club back low and flat around your body? If so, you're likely a low swinger.

The swings of low swingers tend to be very inside out on the downswing with a lot of hand rotation on the club (see figure 7.7). These are short swings that accelerate through the ball very quickly. Most of them play from a closed stance with their bodies back behind the ball through impact.

I think all of these players hit hooks; most of them have built right to left into their swings. I would also call some of the players in this group "fast swingers." As you watch them, their swings appear to be short, fast, and flat. You don't see any long, fast swingers. A good example of a slow, high swinger is Bob Murphy. If you have a long, high swing, you have to have a slow change of direction. In particular, Bob has a very slow transition at the top, which is required for the high swinger. This gives him time to get his swing in position to come down. John Daly is another high swinger who

Figure 7.6 Sherie Steinhauer's high swing makes it necessary for her to slide her hips on the downswing. Note the open clubface at the top, which results from her high right elbow. She gets her power from the high arc.

Figure 7.7 Tommy Armour III shows a low swing that produces a lot of hard action. Notice that keeping his elbow close to his side produces a closed clubface at the top.

has a lot of "wait" in his hips. Unlike the low swinger, the slowing down of the hips on the downswing gives him time for his arms to catch up.

One very distinguishing characteristic of both high and low swingers is the difference in finish position. Low swingers tend to end in an I position (see figure 4.29a on page 108), while high swingers tend to end in a C (see figure 4.29b on page 108) position due to their hard-driving leg action.

Late Releasers

Swings can be classified according to the release of the club. Some players release the club early, and some release it late. The average golfer releases the club too early or casts the club from the top, so most players should strive for a later release. The typical PGA Tour player releases the club very late and maintains his left arm–clubshaft angle far into the downswing. This is because average players use more hand and arm action in their swings, and top PGA professionals use more body action. The average player who casts the club from the top with his hands and arms would be well advised to make a better shoulder turn, shorten the swing at the top, and bring the swing down with his lower body starting first. This gives him or her a later release, and, thus, more distance.

If you can bend one hand back with the other until it is at a right angle to your forearm, then you have enough flexibility to be a late releaser. You will find that if you have flexible hands and wrists you will be able to delay the club. If you don't, then an earlier release will be better suited to you.

Generally speaking, if you need more distance, try working on a later release. You'll find that smaller golfers get a lot of their power from a late release. A good example is Joe Durant on the PGA Tour (see figure 7.8). Other late releasers (also called "diggers") are Brad Faxon, Sergio Garcia, and Steve Flesch (a lefty). All of these golfers maintain the left arm–clubshaft angle far into their downswing and create their power this way. They are called diggers because their severe left arm–clubshaft angle gives them a

Figure 7.8 Joe Durant, one of the best ball strikers on the tour, shows his late release.

steep approach to the ball and then the turf. Late releasers tend to be very good iron players but only average drivers. Also, if you are a better driver than an iron player, work on more lag to help your iron play. It will help you strike down on the ball, create more clubhead angle, and transfer more spin on the ball. The spin will give you more control over the ball.

One warning about the late release—it can be very tricky for some amateurs and recreational players. In fact, even for the pros the complicated swing mechanics of a late release haven't always proven to be a good thing. It's a very high-maintenance mechanic and can abandon players when they most need it. The late release has a lot to do with exceptional feel and timing. It is also extremely important to keep your hands soft. This style can generate a lot of clubhead speed, but some golfers build so much lag into their downswings that they have difficulty controlling the speed of the clubhead at impact, especially with their wedges. Golfers who have too much lag in their swing often hit the ball to the right.

Don't get me wrong—delaying the release in the downswing is generally a good thing. But sometimes too much of a good thing will hurt your swing. While a little lag in the downswing is good, too much lag is difficult to control and makes the precision of the swing very difficult to maintain, which is why these players have more problems in their short games from time to time. Steve Flesch is one of the late releasers I have worked with from time to time. In my opinion, Steve has a better downswing than most late releasers because his backswing is shorter and wider, which helps him widen his downswing.

Try the following two drills to learn how to delay your release:

- Delay drill: Simply hold a club with your left hand only as you pull back on the shaft with your right hand. This drill will help you learn the feel of not casting the right hand and club outward.

- Towel drill: Put a towel on the end of your driver and swing normally. The weight of the towel will create a later release (refer back to figure 4.18 on page 98).

Early Releasers

Early releasers are what I call "sweepers," most of whom are very accurate ball strikers. The early release is a very accurate way to play because the left arm and clubshaft are all lined up at impact, and there are no angles to manipulate at the bottom. These players tend to be extremely accurate drivers and wedge players (whereas late hitters tend to be exceptional iron players). As I've mentioned, however, most average players on courses in America tend to learn an early release. The reason for this is the turf is so good that the ball is perched up on the grass. This encourages a sweeping motion. As players get better, they learn a late release by keeping their wrists cocked far into the downswing. This gives them more distance and the ability to reach long par 4's in 2.

An early release also can be defined as a wide downswing whereas a late release can be called a narrow downswing. You can mark this one down and put it into your notebook: The best drivers of the ball on tour have wide downswings (see figures 7.9 and 7.10). For one thing, they have the left arm, left wrist, and clubshaft all lined up in a straight line at impact. There are no difficult and compensating angles to maintain. The wide downswing squares the clubhead and produces the effective loft of the clubface. The wide downswing is an accurate way to play because the left arm and clubshaft are lined up at impact; there are no angles to manipulate at the bottom (see figure 7.11). The lower-ranking drivers in the statistic charts have narrow, inside, and steep downswings. I really work at getting the average player to understand that even at the professional level, players are typically better iron players or drivers and are rarely equally adept at both. Obviously, the tour players are pretty good with all of their shots or they wouldn't be on the tour, but they all tend to be either better drivers and short-game players or better iron players. This is because narrow swingers with a lot of clubshaft angle will be good iron players but will struggle with their drives. Conversely, a wider downswing with less left arm–clubshaft angle will be great for drivers and wedge players.

Nick Faldo and Nick Price both used to have narrow downswings. Working with top instructor David Leadbetter, they widened their downswing

Figure 7.9 Lee Trevino, a Champions Tour player, is a late releaser but widens his downswing right before impact.

Figure 7.10 Stuart Appleby shows a wide downswing.

Figure 7.11 Notice how the left arm, club-shaft, and clubhead are all in a straight line at impact—an example of an accurate player.

and became much more accurate drivers of the ball, as well as better pitchers of the ball. It's a tradeoff—when you widen the downswing you lose distance but gain accuracy. So, if you need accuracy over distance, then try to widen your downswing. If you need distance, try to narrow your swing with a late release.

Open-Face Releasers

Johnny Miller was an outstanding iron player in his prime and very much of an open clubface player. Other outstanding ball strikers who kept the clubface open to the swing plane most of the way through the swing are Corey Pavin, John Cook, and Steve Flesch. There are a lot of open clubface players on the tour. Players in this category base the timing of their swing on the clubface being open on the backswing, at the top (or vertical at the top, see figure 7.12), and then squaring up the blade very quickly through impact. Most of these players have weak grips that allow them to open the clubface through the backswing and keep it open at the top with the toe pointing down at the ground. They use more hand and arm rotation on the backswing and not as much body rotation. They tend to hang back on the downswing and hit off their right side (see figure 7.13). Because their clubface is open on the downswing, they usually square the blade with their hands, arms, and upper body, not their legs. Some open-face players, Hal Sutton and John Cook, tend to get on top of the ball more. But you can see this to some extent in all open-face players. The clubface remains open on the downswing, and then they have a choice to make. They must either rotate the hands and arms to release the clubface through the hitting area and hit a hook, or really bow their hands forward to keep the blade square through impact and try to fade the ball. Either way, that's a lot of compensation to make when the clubface is traveling at that speed, and there's plenty of room for error. One of Johnny Miller's main swing objectives at impact was to feel as if his right palm were facing down prior to impact. He had to do this to square his open face.

Figure 7.12 An open face at the top of the swing.

Figure 7.13 Corey Pavin, an open-face player, uses more hand and arm action and less leg action to square the blade.

Johnny Miller and Ben Hogan would bow the left wrist and maintain their wrist set through impact to square the blade, a technique called "hooding" the club. Average players are going to release the hands and arms and hit a big draw because they don't have the hand and arm strength to hold the wrist set through impact. Johnny and Ben had very strong hands and upper arms that allowed them to use this technique.

Johnny and Ben supinated their wrists in order to square up the clubface. They both had very fast-turning hips through impact in order to stop a hook. If they didn't supinate their wrists, the ball would go to the right. They were both very straight and exceptional iron players. Steve Flesch also plays like this. He has a weak grip to stop a hook, a very open face at the top, fast-turning hips through impact, and a supinated right wrist at impact. Steve is a wonderful ball striker. In my opinion, he has the best swing on the PGA Tour. His swing is well worth modeling after if he matches your style.

Generally speaking, if you tend to be mainly a hands and arms player, not using your body much on your backswing or downswing, you're likely an open-face player. Of course, because you're not using your body, the power you can attain is more limited than body players can achieve. But you might have shot-making potential. If you're suspecting you're an open-face player, watch for tour players who tend to keep their weight more evenly distributed with slower turning hips through impact. Sometimes they look as if they're on their right leg when they're striking the ball, which allows them to release the club with their hands and arms through impact. Watch for this characteristic and the others I've mentioned, and try to determine if you qualify as an open-face player. If so, there are many players on the tour to view closely as you try to find a match.

Shut-Face Blockers and Shut-Face Releasers

Figure 7.14 A closed face at the top of the swing.

This player uses a strong grip, like Paul Azinger or David Duval. The ball is played back farther in the stance than most styles of play to offset the strong grip. The stance is generally open or aimed left of the target. The backswing is flat and around the body. The club closes to the swing arc on the backswing mainly because of the strong grip and low swing plane. The clubface points up to the sky at the top (closed face), as shown in figure 7.14.

As the downswing starts, shut-face blockers and releasers try to open the clubface or, at the least, get it back to a square position. They do this by tilting the right side back and driving the legs toward the target. This side bending is very hard on the back and not recommended unless you are in excellent physical shape. Every shut-face player I've observed has back problems from time to time.

Additional Customization Options

If you have followed me to this point in the book you now know that there's no one best way to swing a golf club—but there are certainly some fundamentals to follow. One of the basic themes of this book is that you should swing the way your body allows you to swing. Your levels of strength and flexibility have much to do with how you should swing.

In the sections that follow, I've outlined five groups and some fundamentals they should follow in their swings. If you fall into any of these groups (if you're a woman, for example, or if you have a bad back), be sure to read the pertaining information to see how it might apply to your swing.

Swing Modifications for Women

I'm often asked, "Do you teach women the same way you teach men?" My answer is no. I don't teach anyone the same as anyone. That said, women golfers in general do have their own strengths that many men players lack, so I look for these traits first. Women, for example, tend to be strong in the legs and generally very flexible. Men are strong in the upper body and generally not as flexible. Many women have weak wrists, so they must have strong grips (see page 39) when they start (left hand turned to their right). Their strong left-hand grip and long left thumb (see figure 7.15) allow them to set their wrists a little earlier (see figure 7.16) than their male counterparts.

Most women should have strong grips and early wrist sets. I always make sure that the posture is bent forward enough to get the arms past the chest.

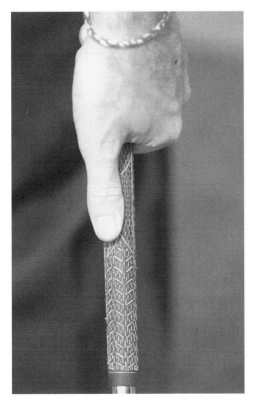

Figure 7.15 A long left thumb on the grip.

Figure 7.16 Rosie Jones shows an early wrist set, a power accumulator for the ladies.

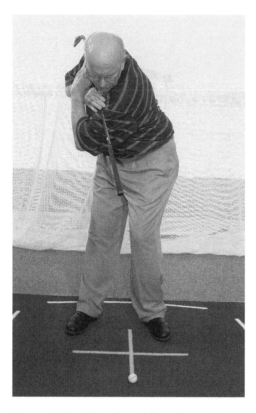

Figure 7.17 The pivot drill performed over stable legs to teach how to turn the shoulders.

I encourage women to put their left arm on top of the chest instead of to the side of the chest, which allows the arms and chest to move together on the takeaway. Although women are very strong in the legs, many have unstable hips on the backswing. They tend to sway their hips. To add stability to the hips, I generally have women hit balls with a stool between their legs (see figure 6.47 on page 171 for an example of this technique). I also tell them to play out of wide stances to further stabilize their lower body.

An attribute many women share is very long swings. Usually, their flexibility allows them to turn more than men, and so the long swing comes naturally to them. To shorten up their swing, I'll make sure they turn their shoulders over stable legs. Also, once their shoulders stop turning, the arms should stop. This will keep the swing shorter. Often, I ask them to do the pivot drill (see figure 7.17), which teaches them the correct rotation of the body over a stable lower body. To perform the pivot drill, cross your arms and hold a club across your shoulders, bend forward in your golf posture, and turn your shoulders until the butt end of the club points a foot outside the ball. Come through, turn your chest at the target, and point the other end of the club outside the ball.

The majority of women have been told to use their arms on their downswing and to forget about using their legs. But if they heed this advice, they take their strength (their legs) out of their swing. I encourage them to start their downswing with their hips, not their arms. This allows them to open up their hips at impact (see figure 7.18) and double their power.

Finally, most women need clubhead speed at impact. To develop this, I have them do the swoosh drill and the tee-to-tee drill. To perform the swoosh drill, turn your club upside down and swing the club, listening for the "swoosh" through impact. Do it with both hands and with the left hand only. This seems to aid women in developing their clubhead speed and proper release of their hands.

To perform the tee-to-tee drill, put a tee in the grip end of a golf club. Now, on the backswing, point the tee at the ball. This drill teaches the proper cocking and uncocking of the wrist (see figure 7.19).

Figure 7.18 LPGA player Donna Andrews opens up her hips at impact to get her power.

Figure 7.19 The tee-to-tee drill for a proper release of the hands. Point the club at the ball both back and through.

These drills teach women to cock their wrists early and recock and release their wrists immediately after impact. This is important because women generally don't release the club very well through impact. I also use the split-grip drill to demonstrate the correct hand and arm release through impact (see figure 7.20). In using the split-grip drill there should be about four inches (10 centimeters) between both hands. Now, just turn the hands over through impact.

Figure 7.20 The split-grip drill helps women feel the release of the hands and arms through impact.

In summary, there are three common errors that many women make in their swings:

- **Hip sway.** Most women sway their hips on the backswing (see figure 7.21). This locks out the right leg and stops their shoulders from turning. To stop this I have them put their right knee against an obstacle as they swing the club (see figure 7.22). I also ask them to keep their right leg flexed as they turn the left shoulder over the right leg.

- **Long, high overswing.** In my experience, most women golfers overswing (see figure 7.23). I believe this happens because they are trying for more power. I try to stop the overswing by stabilizing the legs on the backswing and lowering and shortening the swing by having women do the hook-coil drill without a club. Simply get into your golf posture and hook your right hand in front of your left. Turn and coil the shoulders, keeping the left arm straight (see figure 7.24).

- **Chicken wing.** The chicken wing (see figure 7.25) is caused by overswinging on the backswing and then starting down with the arms instead of the lower body. This leaves the golfer's weight on the back leg and she scoops up on the ball. To banish the chicken wing, the golfer must shorten her swing and eliminate the hip sway going back. Then, she must start down with her lower body, not the hands and arms. To help women get rid of this problem, I have them hit into an impact bag to feel the hands be ahead of the clubhead at impact (see figure 7.26).

Figure 7.21 LPGA player Louise Davis demonstrates a hip sway.

Figure 7.22 Place your right leg against an obstacle to stop hip sway.

Figure 7.23 Example of an overswing.

Figure 7.24 Hook-coil drill at the top.

Figure 7.25 The chicken wing at impact.

Figure 7.26 Hit into an impact bag to practice getting the hands ahead of the club at impact.

Swing Modifications for Women

- Strong grip, long left thumb
- Bent-over posture
- Wider than normal stance
- Upper arms on top of the chest, not to the side
- Low hands at address
- Early wrist set and right-elbow fold on backswing
- Lower body quiet without much hip turn on backswing

- Left foot on ground at top
- Lower, shorter swing
- Stable legs on backswing
- Hips and legs start downswing
- Swing more inside-out through impact
- Release hands and arms through impact
- High, balanced finish

Swing Modifications for Seniors

As we get on in years, we see and feel our flexibility and strength diminish. Our once long, parallel swing at the top gets to only a three-fourths position. Our drives get shorter, our back gets sorer, our knees sometimes ache . . . but of course we still want to play. What's the answer?

If you're a senior player, you will probably derive most of your power from your hands and arms. Your grip should be strong or turned to your right. Your stance should be narrow, with both feet flared out—this makes it easier to turn your body. The ball should be played back a little farther in the stance, and you should probably close up the stance for the driver to get a bigger turn. Because the senior swing is shorter (as a result of less flexibility), you should set your wrists a little earlier on the backswing, which will add leverage to your swing. I also encourage seniors or other golfers without a lot of flexibility to take the club inside the target line on the backswing to make it easier to turn the shoulders.

Your hips should turn freely on the backswing, with the left heel coming off the ground. Your wrists might be a little cupped at the top to get a complete wrist cock and add leverage in your swing. You should also go ahead and bend your left arm a little. You can't turn your shoulders, so bending this arm will get you more arc. Your swing might be a little flat because of normal deterioration of flexibility in the torso. To offset this, turn your hips as much as you can. I encourage all seniors to swing a weighted club to help maintain the length of their arc and the quality of their shoulder turn.

Your downswing should start with the lower body as your weight shifts to the left side. Your arms come down inside the target line as your hands release aggressively through impact. This is a very inside-outside swing with a hooking action. The finish is erect to take pressure off the back.

Swing Modifications for Seniors or Golfers With Low Flexibility

- Don't bend over—stand up tall
- Strong grip, hold club lightly
- Closed stance (aimed to the right)
- Ball more in center of the stance
- Take club inside on takeaway with early wrist set
- Swing low at top
- Left heel off ground on backswing to allow hips to turn
- Left arm bent and left wrist cupped at top
- Let head rotate to the right with the shoulder turn
- Allow right arm and elbow to get away from the body at the top
- Let hips and body come down in an all-together motion
- Finish straight and in balance with your body

Swing Modifications for Juniors

The junior has no fear. You've heard the saying, "To play golf well, you need the mind of a child"? That sentiment applies here. Juniors are great imitators. They just copy Tiger Woods and Ernie Els. They have very little strength in their hands, arms, or wrists but quite a bit of strength in their legs. Much like women players, they are very flexible.

In general, I encourage juniors to play very naturally until they mature. The natural swing for juniors usually includes a strong but full-fingered grip. They should also play out of a wide stance to stabilize the legs. The ball will be forward to accommodate fast leg action. Young players will generally pick the club up with their hands and wrists because they don't have the strength in the wrists to use a conventional one-piece takeaway. The swing is generally long because of the level of flexibility. Junior players tend to take the club back long because of the loose leg action on the backswing. The downswing is all body action. Usually, juniors drive their hips and legs so hard on the downswing that it looks as if their legs and hips are wide open at impact and their arms are way back and trying to catch up. This is the junior player's strongest part of his or her body stealing the show. At the finish, balance seems to be a problem. Work on the junior player's balance by forcing him or her to hold the finish for three to five seconds.

Swing Modifications for Juniors

- Use shorter, lighter clubs
- Strong grip, hold club lightly
- Wide stance
- Stand taller
- Ball forward in stance
- Early set on backswing
- Keep left foot planted on backswing
- Use long, loose, natural swing
- Legs quiet on backswing
- Use legs on downswing
- Hold balance for five seconds at finish

Swing Modifications for Tall Men

Are you a big man? I'm referring to you here only if you're 77 inches (196 centimeters) or taller. You have long legs and long arms, and your center of gravity is way up there. Unfortunately, this makes even the slightest error in movement a real problem. My first suggestion if you're a player of this body type is that you get longer, more upright clubs. In your setup, you need to bend forward from the hips to supplement a significant knee flex. (Basically, the taller you are, the more knee flex you must have.) You should stay very centered on your backswing. Don't sway to the right or move off the ball in your backswing—this could be a disaster. To take advantage of your height, your swing should be wide and high. Try to keep your knees stable on the backswing. Minimize your tendency to slide your legs too much on the downswing. Just turn your hips. A slide will throw your swing into an extremely inside-out pattern, and you'll hook or push the ball.

Work on your balance. Many tall people have balance problems because of their tendency to sway. Your big arc should be used to your advantage but, overall, try to stay very centered with your head and just turn around your spine. Remember that the slightest movement right or left or up or down will be magnified because of your height.

Swing Modifications for Tall Men

- Use more than normal knee flex
- Bend from the hips forward quite a bit
- Use a wide stance
- Keep head very steady throughout the movement
- Use a wide, one-piece takeaway
- Use a high swing to take advantage of your height
- Keep legs quiet on backswing as shoulders turn
- Eliminate excessive slide with legs on downswing
- Make balance a priority

Swing Modifications for a Bad Back

Although golfers incur many injuries through wear and tear and the repetitive nature of their movements, by far the most common complaint is back pain. Eighty percent of all golfers incur back problems at some time during their career. Most of these problems will go away through exercise, rest, and physical therapy, but many of them keep coming back. If you have chronic back problems and would like to play without pain, here is an alternate way to swing.

What moves in the golf swing may cause undue pressure on the spine and discs? The first answer is your posture. When you bend over from the hips with a straight spine, you might feel some pain—if you do, you're like a lot of people. If you have a bad back, my first tip is to stand taller at the spine and flex your knees a bit more than you're used to doing (see figure 7.27). Standing taller might require longer, more upright clubs, so be prepared to buy new clubs.

Other potential spine stressors include keeping your head steady on the backswing, coiling your shoulders and your hips, and turning too much at the spine. Many of these movements are actually suggested by people trying to *help* you with your back. But these kinds of tips that you hear from club pros and other people probably do more harm than good. While I'm on this topic, I can't tell you how many times students have told me that they've been instructed to widen their stance if they have a bad back. The vast majority of times, this is a simple case of misinformation—the width of your stance should be narrow to make it easier to turn your hips.

If you have a bad back, you should play out of a very narrow stance with both feet flared outward (see figure 7.28). The narrow stance allows your hips to turn freely. Your stance should also be slightly closed to allow for an easy turn of the body. Play the ball in the center of your stance. Your posture should be erect with a considerable amount of knee flex. Your grip should be on the strong side because you'll be using your hands and arms more than your body at impact.

Figure 7.27 A more erect posture and a longer club are good for the golfer with a bad back.

Figure 7.28 A narrow stance with both feet flared out.

Four turns occur during the back-swing. If you have a bad back, these turns will ideally happen at the same time. The head turns (and should rotate a little), the shoulders turn, the hips turn, and the knees turn. When the knees turn, the left foot should come off the ground. When everything turns together on the backswing, there's no coil. It's the coil that puts pressure on the back.

Try to keep your backswing short. A long swing generally causes the spine to tilt back toward the target. Don't drive your legs hard on the downswing—hospital beds are full of leg drivers. When you drive your legs from the top of the swing, your upper body has to tilt backward, which stresses your back. Your downswing should be an all-together type of movement. Just as everything moved together on the backswing, everything should move together coming down.

Golfers with bad backs should not try to keep the head steady on the backswing—this puts a lot of stress on the spine. Also, trying to keep your head down at impact is a back wrecker. Just let your head rotate toward the target with the momentum of the swing as you come through. Modern instruction also recommends a lot of side bending to the right on the downswing. I would get rid of this potential back wrecker and replace it with a feeling that your upper body is getting on top of the quiet legs on the downswing.

Be sure not to open up your hips if you have a bad back. Just keep your feet on the ground at impact and let the momentum of the swing bring the right foot off the ground at the finish. Your belt buckle should be facing the ball at impact with both feet on the ground. Your knees should stay bent at impact, as they were throughout the swing. If your knees straighten out any time during your swing, your back will be stressed.

Let your head move after impact. Golfers who keep their heads down too long after impact almost certainly stress the spine. Watch Annika Sorenstam and try to let your head move like hers at impact. This will relieve pressure on your back. Finally, finish erect in the I position, not in the C position (see figures 4.29, a-b on page 108). Let your head come up and out of the shot—don't stay down and back.

Swing Modifications for Golfers With Bad Backs

- Use longer, more upright clubs
- Stand erect with plenty of knee flex
- Ball in center of stance with head behind the ball
- Strong grip to ensure hand action through impact
- Closed stance to make turn easier
- Very narrow stance with both feet flared
- Take club back inside the target line with one-piece takeaway
- Turn hips, shoulders, and head together on backswing—no coil
- Keep arm swing short on backswing
- Left foot rises on backswing
- Upper body feels like it is coming over the top on downswing (outside-inside)
- Legs quiet on downswing, no leg drive
- Eliminate side bending to the right on downswing
- Both feet flat on ground at impact with belt buckle facing ball
- Release hands and arms hard through impact
- Finish very erect with head in front of left leg

Equipment Considerations

Golfers at all skill levels can dramatically improve their ball-striking skills by having properly fitted equipment. Not only do they help in learning the fundamentals, but they can make the difference in perfecting the nuances of the game. The following discussion provides some brief equipment considerations.

Women

Most women should play with a 5-iron through a sand wedge and lob wedge. I wouldn't recommend any long irons, but I prefer replacing them with a utility club. The more woods you use the better; the woods seem to accommodate your sweeping motion—1 to 7-woods are good choices. Additionally, ladies should play with lightweight steel shafts or even graphite. I would also recommend clubs that are perimeter and bottom weighted. This combined with the lightweight shaft helps to get the ball up in the air. Grips should be soft and thin to allow for a better release and since most women are slow swingers, you need a flexible shaft. A low kick shaft is also best for women because it helps get the ball up in the air. Finally, look for woods and irons that are offset near the hosel. This helps you hook the ball.

Seniors

Like the ladies, seniors should find a shaft that is long with a low flex point. The extra kick in the shaft will help you get the ball up in the air and give you an increased distance. Stick with graphite shafts because they tend to be extra light and flexible. You might also want a driver with 13 or 14 degrees loft. This will also help to get the ball up in the air.

A few other tricks of the trade for seniors are as follows:

- If you have arthritis in the hands and wrists, an oversize grip may help.
- Carry more scoring clubs and fewer distance clubs. I recommend 4 wedges. There are a variety of utility clubs on the market to choose from.
- Avoid carrying long irons. Use the ½-wood, ½-iron combination to replace your 3- and 4-iron. This utility club looks like a wood with a small bottom to it. Most of the weight is close to the bottom of the club so it helps the club get up in the air.
- All of your clubs should be slightly offset. This helps you hook the ball if you are a slicer.
- Use a hooked face with your driver with plenty of loft.

Juniors

Juniors need shorter clubs to accommodate their height and strength. Light-weight shafts are also a good choice. Unfortunately, many junior clubs don't fit them. Many of them play with cut down shafts that are too stiff and feel too light. The junior golfer must be able to feel some weight in the clubhead in order to learn a correct swing.

The set makeup for a junior should include a driver and 3-wood. In the irons I would add a 5, 7, 9 pitching wedge and sand wedge. The clubs should be light but balanced with grips that are small in order to learn the correct hold on the club.

For each of these groups, I cannot emphasize the need to get fitted correctly when buying or adding to your set of clubs. To ensure you have the right fit, go to a qualified club fitter each time you're ready to expand your set.

Conclusion

I hope after reading these pages, you're eager to make some changes in your swing. But as you prepare to bring a fresh, more enlightened beginning to your search for the customized swing that works best for you, I ask you to have patience. It's sad but true that few things worth having come quickly. You have hours and hours of work ahead of you (if anything involving the game of golf can be called work) as you practice training your powers of perceptiveness and analysis. Above all, remember the following key points—study the mechanics of the sound swing, build your swing around solid fundamentals within a natural style that works for you, and then fine tune your natural abilities through drilling and practice.

Let your ball flight be your teacher. As you learn your fundamentals, make room for feel and some compensations. Try to stay with your dominant power source as you model your swing after a similar body type.

Remember, all swings are different but try to stay within those fundamentals that are common to all swings. Once you have matched up your fundamentals with your body type, swing style, and preferred ball flight, you are getting close to finding your perfect swing. Enjoy your search and remember, the fun is in the search—learning anything is not a destination but a journey.

Note: The italicized *f* and *ff* following page numbers refer to figures and multiple figures, respectively.

About the Author

Jim Suttie has a doctor of arts degree with a concentration in biomechanics from Middle Tennessee State University. Known as the teacher's teacher and teacher of the pros, he has 36 years of experience in golf instruction. Suttie has taught more than 150 PGA, LPGA, and Champions Tour professionals including Chip Beck, Fred Funk, Carin Koch, Vicki Goetze-Ackerman, Steve Flesch, Silvia Cavalleri, Loren Roberts, Tom Purtzer, and Paul Azinger. On an international level, Suttie has worked with golfers on every world tour including the European Tour, Japanese Tour, and Asian Tour, and he is presently a consultant for the Dutch Federation.

Upon completion of his doctorate, Suttie went on to study how the body is designed to function, incorporating his years of practical experience with his academic background to develop the best method for golfers to achieve the perfect swing. He is also credited with bringing the use of high-speed video to golf instruction.

Suttie is a *Golf Magazine* Top 100 teaching professional and was one of *Golf Digest*'s Top 50 Teachers in the USA for the 2005-06 season. He was also named the 2000 National PGA Teacher of the Year. He is also a three-time recipient of the Illinois PGA Teacher of the Year award and was named the PGA National Teacher of the Year in 2000. Suttie writes regularly for *Golf Magazine*, *Golf Digest*, and *Golf Tips*. He has been seen frequently on the Golf Channel, is a member of the PGA Teaching Summit, and conducts numerous seminars for the PGA. Suttie's Web site is www.JimSuttie.com.

Suttie lives in Bonita Springs, Florida, with his wife, Sandra.